Job Interview Questions Series

Hibernate, **Spring** **& Struts**

Interview Questions
You'll Most Likely Be Asked

378
Interview Questions

Hibernate, **Spring & Struts**

Interview Questions You'll Most Likely Be Asked

ISBN-10: 1-946383-02-3
ISBN-13: 978-1-946383-02-0

Library of Congress Control Number: 2011920203

Vibrant Publishers books are available at special quantity discount for sales promotions, or for use in corporate training programs. For more information please write to **bulkorders@vibrantpublishers.com**

Please email feedback / corrections (technical, grammatical or spelling) to **spellerrors@vibrantpublishers.com**

To access the complete catalogue of Vibrant Publishers, visit **www.vibrantpublishers.com**

Table of Contents

Hibernate

Spring

Dear Reader,

Thank you for purchasing **Hibernate, Spring & Struts Interview Questions You'll Most Likely Be Asked.** We are committed to publishing books that are content-rich, concise and approachable enabling more readers to read and make the fullest use of them. We hope this book provides the most enriching learning experience as you prepare for your interview.

Should you have any questions or suggestions, feel free to email us at reachus@vibrantpublishers.com

Thanks again for your purchase. Good luck with your interview!

- Vibrant Publishers Team

facebook.com/vibrantpublishers

This page is intentionally left blank.

Hibernate, **Spring &** **Struts** Interview Questions

Review these typical interview questions and think about how you would answer them. Read the answers listed; you will find best possible answers along with strategies and suggestions.

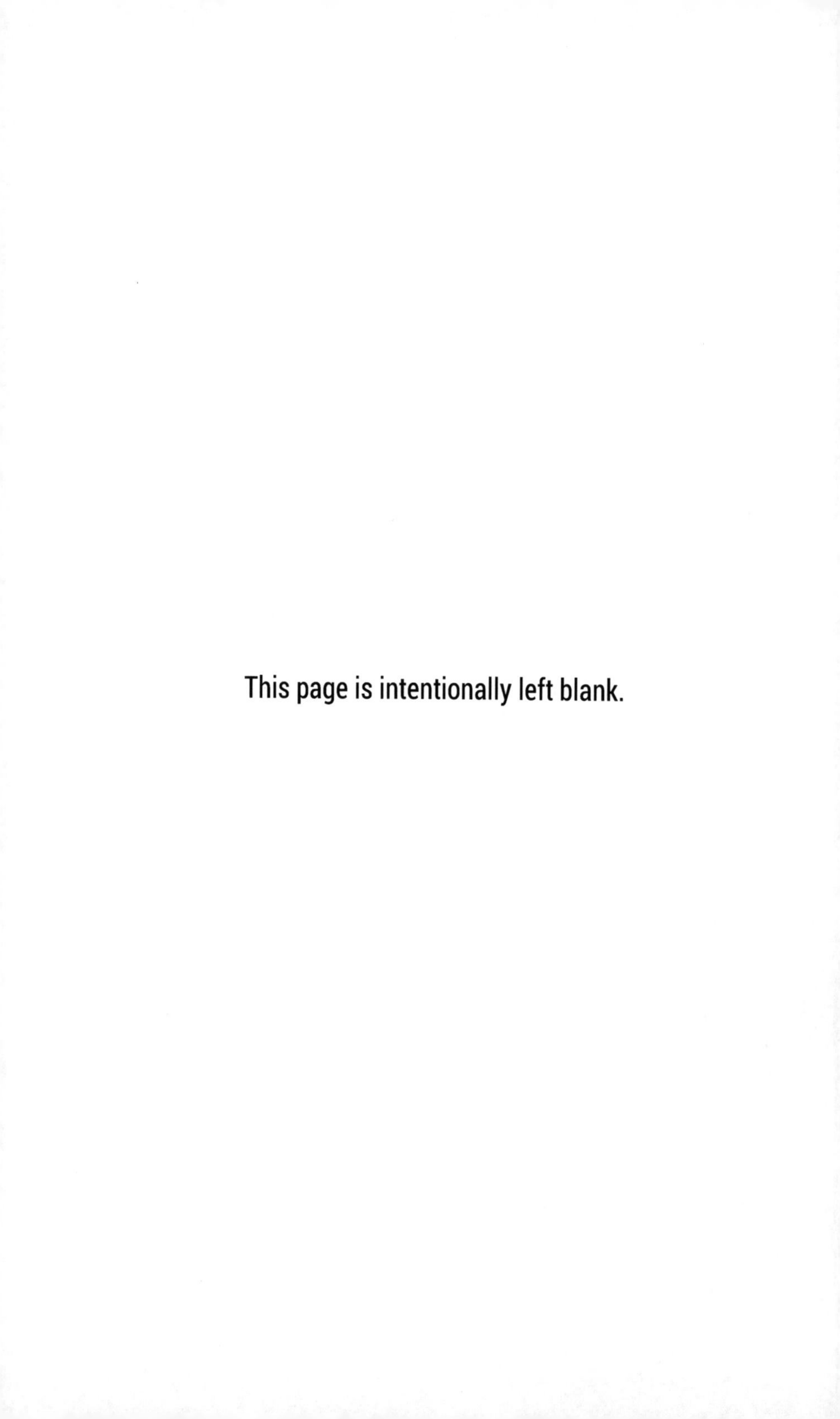
This page is intentionally left blank.

Hibernate

This page is intentionally left blank.

Chapter **1**

Hibernate Interfaces

1: Explain Database Transaction management using Transaction Interface.

Answer:

In Hibernate, every transaction is handled by a session object. It controls the transactions and hides it from the outer world. To make sure the transaction completes successfully and is committed upon success and is rolled back upon failure, the entire transaction happens within a try – catch block. Within the try block, the session begins the transaction and continues with the processes and finally commits it. If anything goes wrong, the try block throws an error and under the exception handling part, a rollback is issued for the transaction. And finally, the session is closed. This is an efficient way of handling database transactions using Hibernate.

2: What are the core interfaces available in hibernate?

Answer:

The core interfaces available in hibernate are:

a) **Session**: used to store and retrieve the objects and they are not thread-safe
b) **SessionFactory**: one object being created per application
c) **Criteria**: used to provide a conditional search over resultset
d) **Query**: obtained by invoking createQuery() method of Session
e) **Configuration**: used to specify the hibernate mapping file's location
f) **Transaction**: used to perform several database operations

3: What is SessionFactory? Is it thread-safe object?

Answer:

SessionFactory is an interface creating session instances. Threads servicing the client requests obtain the session instances from the SessionFactory. SessionFactory is created only once for each application. More than one thread can access the SessionFactory concurrently since it is thread-safe object.

4: How will you create SessionFactory object?

Answer:

SessionFactory object can be created using buildSessionfactory() method.

```
import org.hibernate.SessionFactory;
import org.hibernate.cfg.Configuration;
```

```
SessionFactory sf = new
Configuration().configure().buildSessionFactory();
```

5: What is Session? Is it a thread safe object?

Answer:

Session is obtained from SessionFactory and not thread-safe, meaning that it cannot be shared between threads. It is a single unit of work with the database. To avoid creating multiple sessions, ThreadLocal can be used. Get current session from the ThreadLocal object using get(). If no sessions are available, get a new session from SessionFactory object using openSession() method and set it in ThreadLocal.

6: Explain about Criteria in hibernate.

Answer:

a) Criteria in hibernate are used to create dynamic queries to execute
b) Criteria instances are obtained from session object using createQuery() method
c) Criteria mycriteria = session1.createCriteria(Empl.class)

Chapter 2

Hibernate Configuration

7: How do you configure hibernate?

Answer:

Hibernate could be configured in the following methods:

a) Create hibernate configuration file "hibernate.cfg.xml" to provide hibernate configuration properties
b) Create hibernate mapping file say "emp.hbm.xml" to provide hibernate mapping details i.e., mapping tables and java objects
c) Configuration class uses these two files to create SessionFactory which in turn creates session instances

8: What are the important tags of hibernate configuration file (hibernate.cfg.xml)?

Answer:

The important tags of hibernate configuration file are:

```
<! DOCTYPE ... >
<hibernate-configuration>
    <session-factory>
        <property name="..">  ... </property>
        ...
    </session-factory>
</hibernate-configuration>
```

a) **DTD:** doctype
b) **Configuration of JDBC connection:** driver class, url, username, password
c) **Dialect:** specify the type of sql to be generated
d) **Size of Connection Pool**
e) **Specify hbm2ddl.auto:** automatic generation of database schema
f) **Map hbm.xml files:** include Hibernate Mapping files

9: Why column attribute is required if the property name is "date"?

Answer:

If the column attribute is not given hibernate will map the column -name as the property name. However if "date" is given as property name, column should be explicitly given since date is a keyword.

```
<property name="date" column="created_date"/>
```

10: How will you get hibernate statistics?

Answer:

Hibernate statistics could be obtained by:

a) using getStatistics() method of SessionFactory
b) SessionFactory.getStatistics();

11: How will you make generated sql to be displayed in console?

Answer:

Generated sql could be displayed in console by setting "show_sql" property to "true" in the hibernate configuration file.

<property name = "show_sql" > true </property>

12: How are the columns of the database mapped with the java class properties in hibernate?

Answer:

The columns of the database are mapped with the java class properties in hibernate as follows:

a) Write POJO (getters and setters) class
b) Create hibernate mapping file "hibernate.cfg.xml" where mapping between table columns and the class properties are specified

```
<hibernate-mapping>
    <class name="empl" table="empl_tabl">
        <property name="name" column="empl_name">
        <property name="age" column="empl_age"/>
        <many-to-one name="dept" cascade="all"
        column="dept_Id"/>
    </class>
</hibernate-mapping>
```

13: If you want to insert data for few columns into a large table with hundreds of columns, hibernate will generate the insert sql query at run time containing all the table columns which will create performance issue. How will you make the hibernate to generate dynamically generated sql queries containing only the necessary columns? For instance, it should not include the null columns / property values.

Answer:

We can make the hibernate to generate dynamically generated sql queries using **dynamic-insert="true"** attribute in the class mapping. Default option is "false".

```
<class name=".." table="UserDetails" catalog="ks" dynamic-
insert="true" >
...
</class>
```

14: What is the flow of hibernate communication with database?

Answer:

The flow of hibernate communication with database is as follows:

a) First, load hibernate configuration file and create configuration object. Using configuration object load all hibernate mapping files.
b) Create SessionFactory from the Configuration object.
c) Create Session from the SessionFactory object.
d) Create the HQL query.
e) Run the query which retrieves list of java objects.

15: How will you configure Sequence generated primary key?

Answer:

We can configure sequence generated primary key by using <generator> tag.

```
<id column="emp_Id" name="empId" type="java.lang.Long">
    <generator class="sequence">
        <param name="myseq"> emp_id_seq </param>
    <generator>
</id>
```

16: How will you change one relational database to another database without code changes?

Answer:

We can change a relational database to another using hibernate SQL dialect. Hibernate will generate sql queries based on the dialect defined in the configuration file.

```
<property name="dialect"> org.hibernate.dialect.MySQLDialect
</property>
```

17: What is dynamic-insert and dynamic-update option in the class mapping?

Answer:

Dynamic-insert and dynamic-update option in the class-mapping are:

a) **dynamic-insert="true/false":** Used to decide whether to include the columns having null properties, in the dynamically generated sql INSERT statement
b) **dynamic-update="true/false":** Used to decide whether to include the null columns, in the dynamically generated sql

UPDATE statement

18: How will you configure Hibernate to access the instance variables directly without using setter method?

Answer:

We can configure hibernate to access the instance variables directly without using setter method as follows:

a) Using access="field" attribute in the <property> tag (mapping file)
b) <property name="uname" access="field"/>

19: What is Automatic Dirty checking in hibernate?

Answer:

Automatic Dirty checking in hibernate:

a) means that Hibernate persists the data (or updates the database) automatically if the state of the object is modified inside a transaction when the transaction is committed and the session is opened
b) means no need for explicit update statemen

20: Write down a sample code for Automatic Dirty checking.

Answer:

Automatic Dirty checking Sample Code:

```
Session session1 = sessionFactory1.openSession();
Transaction tx1 = session1.beginTransaction();
    User user = (User)session1.get(User.class, 5L);
    user.setUname("Shobhana");
tx1.commit(); //data is synchronized with database
```

```
session1.close();
```

21: How hibernate is database independent and what are the changes required?

Answer:

Hibernate is database independent as by changing the below properties, databases can be replaced without much changes.

```
<property name="hibernate.dialect">
    org.hibernate.dialect.Oracle9Dialect
</property>

<property name="hibernate.connection.driver_class">
    oracle.jdbc.driver.OracleDriver
</property>
```

22: How will you include hibernate mapping file in the hibernate configuration file?

Answer:

We can include hibernate mapping file in the hibernate configuration file using <mapping> tag and resource attribute.

```
<mapping resource="user.hbm.xml" />
<mapping resource="addr.hbm.xml" />
```

This page is intentionally left blank.

Chapter 3

Criteria Queries

23: What are the ways in which object can be fetched from the database in hibernate?

Answer:

The ways in which object can be fetched from the database in hibernate are:

a) using Criteria API
b) using Standard SQL
c) using HQL
d) using identifier

24: What is the use of Restrictions class?

Answer:

Restrictions class is used to implement comparison operations in criteria query. Using add() method of criteria query object, Restrictions can be added to the criteria query.

```
Criteria mycriteria = session1.createCriteria(Student.class);
mycriteria.add ( Restrictions.eq("age", 18) );
```

25: How will you write criteria query to retrieve records having dept_name containing "hr" and emp_salary between 20000 and 30000?

Answer:

The required criteria query can be written as follows:

```
List Employees = session1.createCriteria(Empl.class)
    .add( Restrictions.like("dept_name", "hr%") )
    .add(Restrictions.between("emp_salary", 20000, 30000) )
    .list();
```

26: How will you sort the employee class in descending order by employee salary using Criteria query?

Answer:

The employee class can be sorted in descending order by employee salary using Criteria query using org.hibernate.criterion.Order class of Criteria API.

```
Criteria mycriteria = session1.createCriteria(Empl.class);
mycriteria.addOrder(Order.desc ( "emp_salary"));
```

27: How will you find out the maximum salary from Employee class?

Answer:

The maximum salary from employee class can be found using org.hibernate.criterion.Projections class which is used to fetch minimum, maximum, average, distinct count of the property values.

```
Criteria mycriteria = session1.createCriteria(Empl.class);
mycriteria.setProjection ( Projections.max("emp_salary") );
```

28: What are the methods available in Projections class?

Answer:

The methods available in Projections class are:

a) **Projections.rowCount():** to fetch total row count of property values
b) **Projections.countDistinct():** to fetch distinct count
c) **Projections.avg():** to fetch average value
d) **Projections.max():** to fetch maximum value
e) **Projections.min():** to fetch minimum value
f) **Projections.sum():** to fetch sum of property values

29: How will you implement pagination using criteria query?

Answer:

We could implement pagination using setFirstResults() and setMaxResults() methods. For instance, fetching records, starting from 20th record and retrieve the next 40 records from the database.

```
Criteria mycriteria = session1.createCriteria(Empl.class);
mycriteria.setMaxResults(20);
mycriteria.setFirstResult(40);
```

30: What are the disadvantages of Criteria query?

Answer:

The disadvantages of Criteria query are:

a) **Performance issue:** No control over hibernate generated query. If the generated query is slow, it will be difficult to tune the query.

b) **Maintenance issue:** Sql queries are written or scattered in java code. If any issues, we need to find out the problematic query in the application. Named queries which are stored in the hibernate mapping file are the best choice.

31: How is the Primary Key created using Hibernate?

Answer:

The primary key in Hibernate is created using <id> tag in hibernate mapping file.

```
<class name=".." table ="..">
    <id name="userId" type="java.lang.String" >
        <column name="user_Id" length="20"/>
        <generator/>
    </id>
</class>
```

32: How do you create hibernate generated Primary Key?

Answer:

Hibernate generated Primary Key is created using <generator> tag which is used to specify how the primary key should be created in the database.

```
<class name=".." table ="..">
    <id name = "addrId" type="java.lang.Integer">
        <column name="addr_id" />
        <generator class="increment" />
    </id>
    </class>
```

Chapter **4**

Persistent Classes

33: What are Tuplizers?

Answer:

A Tuplizer is responsible for creating a known data structure or a class and managing it in Hibernate. The org.hibernate.tuple.Tuplizer interface and its sub-interfaces are responsible for creating a POJO class using its constructor and using its getter and setter methods or the fields directly to inject or retrieve the values. The component could be a data structure, POJO class or a DOM object. There are 2 types of Tuplizers – ComponentTuplizer and EntityTuplizer. The ComponentTuplizer will be responsible for creating components as requested and the EntityTuplizer will be responsible for creating entities. Depending on the requirement, the concerned Tuplizer will be responsible for creating an entity or a component based on its available definition and will use the defined getters and setters to retrieve and set the values.

34: Why can't we declare a Hibernate persistent class as final?

Answer:

Hibernate uses proxies extensively while calling the load () method or during lazy initialization. Java does not support the final classes to be extended or implemented. To create proxies, the class should be non-final. Even though we can declare a Hibernate persistent class as final, it is not recommended as it affects the performance. Even if the class is not final but the methods are, Hibernate cannot make proxies. Since the final methods cannot be overridden, the proxy call might throw a NullPointerException. If you want to make the class final, make sure that you disable proxy generation with @Proxy (lazy-false).

35: What are the best practices that we need to follow while creating Persistent class?

Answer:

The best practices to follow while creating Persistent class are:

a) Write a POJO class and implement default constructor (no-argument and non-public)
b) Give an identifier property (optional) to map with the primary key of the database table
c) Write non final classes to avoid hibernate's proxies feature which depends upon the POJO class. Otherwise disable proxy using lazy="false" (lazy association fetching) explicitly
d) Declare mutators (setters) and accessors (getters) with the

persistent field names

36: How will hibernate instantiate the persistent classes?

Answer:

Hibernate would instantiate the persistent classes using Constructor.newInstance() method.

37: What are the functionalities available for the POJO classes which declare identifier property?

Answer:

The functionalities available for the POJO classes which declare identifier property are:

a) Session.merge()
b) Session.saveOrUpdate()
c) Cascade update or Cascade merge (Transitive reattachment for the detached objects)

38: What are the methods to be overridden in POJO?

Answer:

Equals() and hashCode() methods should be overridden in POJO if,

a) The POJO classes are required to be stored in Set (Many-one/One-Many associations)
b) The POJO classes require using reattachment of detached objects

39: What is meant by Named SQL query?

Answer:

Named SQL query is defined in the hibernate mapping xml file and invoked from java file whenever required.

Mapping XML file:

```
<sql-query name = "userInfo">
    <return alias="user" class="com.java.User"/>
        SELECT user.user_id AS {user.userId},
                    user.user_name AS {user.uname}
        FROM User user WHERE user.name LIKE: uname
</sql-query>
```

Java File:

```
List userList = session.getNamedQuery ("userInfo")
                .setString ("shobhana", uname)
                .setMaxResults (10)
                .list();
```

40: How will you invoke Stored Procedures?

Answer:

We could invoke Stored Procedures using <sql-query> tag defined in hibernate mapping file.

```
<sql-query name="getAllUsers_sp" callable="true">
    <return alias="user1" class="user">
        <return-property name="userId" column="user_id"/>
        <return-property name="uname" column="user_name"/>
        { ? = call getAllUsers() }
    </return>
</sql-query>
```

Chapter **5**

Object States

41: What is the difference between the Transient and Detached states?

Answer:

In Hibernate, an object is in the transient state before it is attached to a session. A transient object is not connected to a session or a database. It still holds the value which may be written into the database when the session is established and the transaction is committed. Otherwise, it may lose its value when overwritten or be garbage collected. An object is in the Detached state when the session is closed. The values are already written to the database and the transaction is committed and the session is closed. But the database values may change since the last session was closed and hence, the detached object would have become stale. But it can reattach later to another session and become persistent.

42: What are the types of instance/object states?

Answer:

The types of instance/object states are:

a) **Persistent:** Data in sync with session object and database
b) **Transient:** Not connected with session and not sync with database
c) **Detached:** Data not in sync with session and database. Previously persistent and currently not associated with any session. For instance, Data used to be persistent however appropriate session was closed and is waiting for another session to make the data sync with database

43: When does an object come to detached state?

Answer:

a) When the session gets closed, an object becomes detached
b) If the data is modified after closing the session, the changes do not have any effect in the database meaning that it will not be in sync with the database

```
Session sess1 = sessionFactory1.openSession();
User u = sess1.get(User.class, userId);
session1.close();// Object is detached

u.setUname("shobhana");// Modify the data

Session sess2 = sessionFactory1.openSession();
Transaction tx1 = sess2.beginTransaction();
sess2.update(u); // Object is re-attached
tx1.commit;
sess2.close();
```

44: How would you reattach the object to the session when the same object has already been loaded into the session?

Answer:

We could reattach the object to the session when the same object has already been loaded into the session by invoking session.merge() method.

45: How will you know the state of the object or whether it is in sync with database?

Answer:

We would know the state of the object or whether it is in sync with database by using <version> property. Hibernate uses this version number to check whether the row has been updated since the last time it was retrieved when the object is being updated/persisted. If the version needs to be updated in terms of timestamp <timestamp> property can be used instead of <version> property.

POJO class:

```
Class User {
    Private String uname;
    ...
    Private long version;
}
```

Hbm.xml:

```
<class name="user" ...>
    <id ...>
    <property name="uname" ../>
    <version name="currVersion" type="long" />
```

</class>`

46: How will you know the state of objects when you use legacy database and the database cannot be altered to add a version column?

Answer:

The state of objects when we use legacy database can be known using optimistic locking in the <class> mapping without version or timestamp properties.

a) **Using optimistic-lock="all" and dynamic-update="true":** Hibernate uses each fields of the persistent object in the WHERE clause to check the state of all fields in a row meaning that to ensure none of the fields are modified in the row before updating it
b) **Using optimistic-lock="dirty":** Hibernate uses only modified columns for optimistic checking

47: How will you prevent concurrent update in hibernate?

Answer:

We can avoid concurrent update in hibernate as follows:

a) Using Version checking/property when more than one thread tries to access the same data at a time
b) It creates a version number for each row update
c) Retrieve the version number while fetching data for update and do the changes. Fetch the version number again while updating the row. If 2 version numbers differ "StaleObjectStateException" will be thrown
d) Steps to configure:

i) Include version field in POJO class
ii) Include version tag in the class mapping
iii) Include version column in the table
iv) Check the version numbers while updating data
v) If exception, error message can be displayed to handle it

48: What are the pros and cons of Detached object?

Answer:

The pros and cons of detached object are:

a) **Pros:** Break up the longer transactions where user requires time to think, into two or more transactions. Detached object is used to carry over the data to the presentation layer and is modified outside the transaction and later reattached to the transaction using another session
b) **Cons:** Objects may hang around in the hibernate cache memory. It is better to discard the detached object and refetch it for the subsequent requests

49: What is the difference between session.get() and session.load()?

Answer:

The difference between session.get() and session.load() are:

a) **Session.get():** Retrieves data from the database immediately. If the data is not available, it will return null value
b) **Session.load():** Returns a proxy and the database will not be hit immediately until the proxy is first invoked. If the

data is not available in the database, it will return ObjectNotFoundEexception

50: What is the difference between session.saveOrUpdate() and session.save()?

Answer:

The difference is:

a) **Session.saveOrUpdate():** Inserts data into database by invoking save() if it does not exist and invoke update() if the primary key is already present
b) **Session.save():** Executes SELECT first to determine whether the primary key is present or not. If it exists, update the data otherwise insert the data

51: Explain about session.update() and session.lock() methods.

Answer:

Both the session.update() and session.lock() methods reattaches the detached object to the session. Session.lock() reattaches the detached object to the session assuming that it is sync with the database. Hence it is best practice to use either update() or saveOrUpdate() methods.

52: Explain about session.update() and session.merge() methods.

Answer:

a) **Update():** Use it , if the session does not contain the persistent object with the same identifier
b) **Merge():** If the modifications needs to be merged without considering the state of the session

Chapter 6

O/R Mapping

53: Explain the different ORM levels.

Answer:

Hibernate supports 4 ORM levels – Pure relational, full object mapping, medium object mapping and light object mapping. Under the pure relational model, the complete application is based on the SQL-based relational mappings and stored procedures. This will include the user interface also. The full object model supports composition, polymorphism, inheritance and persistence. The medium object model supports Object Oriented model with SQL generated at compile-time. The light model makes use of JDBC wherein the entities become the objects as defined by the classes. The light model is the easiest to implement and the most used for less complex applications.

54: What are the types of mapping?

Answer:

The types of mapping are:

a) One-to-one
b) One-to-Many
c) Many-to-one
d) Many-to-Many
e) Component mapping

55: Explain lazy loading in hibernate

Answer:

Lazy loading is a process through which the child objects are loaded only when required. This reduces unnecessary usage of resources. It is done by setting the 'lazy' propery to true or false. The lazy = true | false property is set based on whether you want to load the child object along with the parent object

a) If lazy = true, it will not load child object. It is the Default option
b) If lazy = false, it will load child object

56: What are the fetching strategies?

Answer:

The various fetching strategies are:

a) **fetch="join":** Disabled the lazy loading
b) **fetch="select":** Default; Enabled the lazy loading
c) **fetch="subselect":** Groups the collection into subselect statement
d) **batch-size="n":** Fetching upto "n" number of collections

57: List out the Cascading options available in hibernate.

Answer:

The cascading options available in hibernate are:

a) Save-update
b) Delete
c) Delete-orphan
d) None
e) All

58: How will you enable cascading?

Answer:

Cascading can be enabled by including "cascade" attribute at <set> tag in hibernate mapping file.

```
<set name="user1" cascade="save-update, delete" table="table1" >
    <key>
        <column name="userid" not-null="true" />
    </key>
    <one-to-many class="com.ks.user" />
</set>
```

59: Explain about inverse attribute.

Answer:

Inverse attribute:

a) is used to decide which side is the relationship owner in the collection to manage the relationship
b) includes 'inverse="true | false" in the <set> tag
c) is applicable to One-to-many and Many-to-many relationship

d) decides which side of the collection should update the foreign key

60: What is component mapping?

Answer:

A component is an object/pojo class (say Address) containing default constructor and getters/setters. It is assigned as a value not a reference to another/enclosed class (say Employee). No need of identifier property in the component class. Its properties are placed in the enclosed class's table hence it cannot have primary key field.

```
<class name="com.ks.employee" table ="employee" >
    <id name="empId" ... />
    <property name="eName" ... />

    <component name="Address" class="com.ks.Address">
        <property name="city" .. />
        ...
    </component>
</class>
```

61: How do you make a class and collection as mutable in Hibernate mapping file?

Answer:

We can make a class and collection as mutable in Hibernate mapping file using mutable="true | false" attribute in <class> tag and <set> tag.

```
<class name="com.java.User" table="user" mutable="false" >
```

```
    <set name="ContactNo" mutable="false" >
        ...
    </set>
</class>
```

62: What are the functions by which the entities are loaded and made read-only automatically, if Session.isDefaultReadOnly() method returns true?

Answer:

The functions by which the entities are loaded and made read-only automatically, if Session.isDefaultReadOnly() method returns true are:

a) session.load()
b) session.get()
c) session.merge()
d) Iterating, Scrolling, Executing the HQL Queries and Criteria

63: What is the default access mode of immutable classes in hibernate and how will you change it?

Answer:

a) By default, access mode of immutable classes in hibernate it is read-only
b) To change the default setting - session.setDefaultReadOnly(false); hence the entities/classes loaded by the hibernate are not read-only

64: Explain about mutable class in hibernate.

Answer:

a) **Mutable="true":** By default; Add, Update, Delete operations are allowed to this class.
b) **Mutable="false":** Add and Delete operations are allowed but Update operation will be ignored for this class. However no exception will be thrown.

65: Explain about mutable collection in hibernate mapping file.

Answer:

a) **Mutable="true":** By default; Add, Update, Delete operations are allowed.
b) **Mutable ="false":** Update and 'Cascade Delete All' operations are allowed; Add and delete-orphan operations are not allowed in this collection with exception thrown. For instance, if cascade-delete is enabled, when the parent is deleted, the child will also be deleted

Chapter **7**

Hibernate Inheritance

66: Explain the advantages and disadvantages of implementing inheritance using Single Table Strategy.

Answer:

In the Single Table strategy, all the properties of all the relations go into one single table. While it is the easiest to execute, there will be many NULL columns in the table to deal with. The tables cannot be normalized. It is simple since, there's only one table to deal with. Since all the data is available in a single table, there's no need to join with other tables for data. Because there's a chance of having more than one type of data, there needs to be one column defined as the discriminator column which will decide what kind of data the row contains.

67: Explain the advantages and disadvantages of implementing inheritance using With Table Per Class Strategy.

Answer:

When the inheritance is implemented with Table per Class strategy, there's a table corresponding to every class. The main advantages of this strategy are that you can define Not Null constraints and since every class has a table corresponding to it, there's no need for a discriminator. The disadvantages of this strategy are that, here also the tables are not normalized. Further the container either has to do multiple fetches from the database or use an SQL Union to satisfy a query. This is not a preferred strategy even though it is easy to implement. The main issue here is to maintain the different tables corresponding to each class become very complicated.

68: Explain the advantages and disadvantages of implementing inheritance using With Joined Strategy.

Answer:

When you are implementing inheritance using With Joined Strategy, you are implementing the most normalized tables in the database. Just like Table Per Class strategy, you can define Not Null constraints. But the main disadvantage is that the Joined strategy does not seem to perform as well as the Single Table strategy. Insert, update and delete needs to be done for each subclass while using this strategy whereas while using the single table strategy, a single insert, update and delete will be enough.

69: What are the types of Inheritance models? Explain.

Answer:

The types of inheritance models are:

a) **Table per class hierarchy:**

   i) One table per class hierarchy

   ii) For instance, 1 base class (School), 2 sub classes (Student, Teacher)

   iii) 1 table for 3 classes (1 base and 2 subclasses)

   iv) Classes are differentiated by Discriminator column in the table

   v) Using <subclass> tag and "discriminator-value" attribute

b) **Table per subclass:**

   i) One table per class and the Primary Key column of Base class table will be present in subclass's table as well

   ii) For instance, 3 tables for 3 classes (1 base and 2 subclasses)

   iii) Using <joined-subclass> and <key> attribute

c) **Table per concrete class:**

   i) One table per class and the Base class table columns (common attributes) will be duplicated in all subclass table

   ii) 3 tables for 3 classes (duplicate columns in subclass tables)

   iii) Using <union-subclass> for each subclass table

d) **Table per concrete class using Implicit Polymorphism:**

   i) One table per class

   ii) Base class table columns (common attributes) will be duplicated in all subclass table

   iii) Using <class> tag for each subclass mappings

iv) No need for explicit definition of base class. However Base class properties will be duplicated in subclass table definitions

70: What is unidirectional and bi-directional association in hibernate mapping?

Answer:

For instance, class A HAS-A relationship with class B. That is, object of B is created in A.

a) **Unidirectional:** If class A is queried, information of B cannot be obtained and using B object, information of A cannot be obtained
b) **Bi-directional:** Using either A or B object, information of both classes can be obtained

Chapter 8

Hibernate Caches

71: What is primary/first level cache in hibernate?

Answer:

a) The primary level cache in hibernate is Hibernate's Default cache
b) It associates with the hibernate's Session object
c) It processes the transactions one after another
d) It is used to minimize the number of queries required to be generated within the same transaction
e) That is, it updates all the modification that has been done within the transaction, into the database at the end of the transaction during committing the transaction, instead of updating the database after every modification

72: Explain about Secondary level cache in hibernate.

Answer:

a) The secondary level cache in hibernate associates with the SessionFactory object.
b) The secondary level cache in hibernate loads the objects into SessionFactory so that the objects will be available to the entire application rather than to be bound for single session.
c) If an object which is already available in the sessionfactory level is returned from the query, it can be used directly from sessionfactory level and no need to go for database transaction. Query cache can also be used here.

73: List out the secondary level cache providers.

Answer:

The various secondary level cache providers are:

a) **EHCache (Easy Hibernate Cache):** Supports read-only and read-write caching
   i) Supports disk-based and memory based caching
   ii) Doesn't support clustering
b) **JBoss Tree Cache:** Supports transactional cache
c) **OSCache (Open Symphony Cache):** Supports read-only and read-write caching
   i) Supports disk-based and memory based caching
   ii) Support clustering via JMS
d) **Swarm Cache:** Supports read-only and Nonstrict read-write caching
   i) Support cluster based caching
   ii) Used for applications/data that has more READ operations than the WRITE operations

74: How will you enable secondary level cache?

Answer:

Secondary level cache can be enabled using "hibernate.cache.use_second_level_cache" property in hib.cfg.xml file.

```
<property name="hibernate.cache.use_second_level_cache">
    true
</property>
```

75: How will you configure the secondary level cache?

Answer:

The steps to configure the secondary level cache are:

a) Activate it by defining "hibernate.cache.provider_class" property in the hibernate configuration file
b) Secondary level cache is activated by default and uses EHCache provider

```
<hibernate-configuration>
    <session-factory>
            ...
        <property name="hibernate.cache.provider_class">
            org.hibernate.cache.EHCacheProvider
        </property>
        ...
    </session-factory>
</hibernate-configuration>
```

76: What are different ways to disable the secondary level cache?

Answer:

The different ways to disable secondary level cache are:

a) Using "use_second_level_cache" property
   <property name="use_second_level_cache"> false </property>
b) Using CACHEMODE.IGNORE in the code
   session.setCacheMode (CACHEMODE.IGNORE);
c) Using "org.hibernate.cache.NoCacheProvider" cache provider in "cache.provider_class" property
   <property name="cache.provider_class">
   org.hibernate.cache.NoCacheProvider
   </property>

77: What is query cache?

Answer:

Cache query is:

a) Used for caching the results of the queries that are running frequently with the same parameters and storing the most recent updates of the queries
b) Not default so it needs to be enabled and uses secondary level cache

78: How will you enable query cache?

Answer:

Query cache can be enabled:

a) Firstly, setting the property "hibernate .cache .use _query _cache" to true in the hibernate configuration file
   <property name= "hibernate.cache.use_query_cache"> true </property>

b) Secondly, using setCacheable(true) in the Query

```
Query q = session.createQuery("from Employee e where e.eid=2");
q.setCacheable(true);
```

79: How will you configure custom cache?

Answer:

The steps to configure custom cache are:

a) Write the required customprovider java classes
b) Set the property "hibernate.cache.provider_class" to customprovider class name in the hibernate configuration file

```
<property name="hibernate.cache.provider_class">
    com.ks.MyCustomCacheProviderClass
</property>
```

80: What are the different caching strategies?

Answer:

There are four types of caching strategies: Read-only, Read-write, Nonstrict read-write, Transactional.

81: How will you implement "read-only" cache?

Answer:

Read-only cache implementation:

```
<class name="..." table="..." mutable= "true">
    ...
    <cache usage="read-only"/>
    ...
```

</class>

82: What are the attributes used in <cache> element?

Answer:

The attributes used in <cache> element are:

a) **Usage:** Mandatory; Used to specify the caching strategy
b) **Region**: Optional; Used to specify the second level cache region's name
c) **Include**: Optional; 'include="all | non-lazy" '; "Non-lazy" option is used to specify the entity that has lazy="true" attribute, may not be cached when the attribute level "lazy fetching" option is enabled

83: How will you prevent the persistent objects from being stored in the first level cache and avoid synchronization of this object with the database when session.flush() in invoked?

Answer:

We can prevent the persistent objects from being stored in the first level cache and avoid synchronization of this object with the database when session.flush() in invoked by:

a) Using evict() method of session object
b) Used to remove the object and its collections from the first level cache
c) For instance, if the "emp" object needs to be removed from the first level cache, invoke session.evict(emp)

84: Can you evict all the objects from the first level/session cache and how?

Answer:

Yes, we can evict all the objects from the first level/session cache by invoking session.clear() method.

85: How will you get the statistics/contents of the secondary level cache/query cache?

Answer:

We can get the statistics/contents of the secondary level cache/query cache using getStatistics() and getSecondLevelCacheStatistics() methods.

```
Map secondCacheStatistics = sessFactory1.getStatistics()
    .getSecondLevelCacheStatistics(secCacheRegionName)
    .getEntries();
```

86: How will you enable statistics and keep the cache statistics entries in a readable format?

Answer:

We can enable statistics and keep the cache statistics entries in a readable format using "hibernate.generate_statistics" and "hibernate.cache.use_structured_entries" properties respectively in the hibernate configuration file.

```
<property name = "hibernate.cache.use_structured_entries"> true
</property>
<property name = "hibernate.cache.use_structured_entries"> true
</property>
```

87: How will you refresh the query cache when you expect that the data may have been updated via separate process not

through hibernate?

Answer:

We can refresh the query cache when you expect that the data may have been updated via separate process not through hibernate using setCacheMode(CacheMode.REFRESH) method.

```
List list = session.createQuery("from Empl emp where emp.eid= 2")
    .setCacheable(true)
    .setCacheMode(CacheMode.REFRESH)
    .list();
```

88: How will you evict the objects from the secondary level cache?

Answer:

a) We can evict the objects from the secondary level cache by invoking evict() method of SessionFactory
b) Used to evict the state of the object, entire class, collection instance and the entire collection
c) Collections have to be explicitly evicted from the sessionfactory/second level cache unlike first level cache where session.evict() will evict collections as well

```
sessFact.evict(Empl.class, empId); //evict particular employee
sessFact.evict(Empl.class); //evict the entire Empl object
sessFact.evictCollection("Empl.contactNos", empId); //evict particular collection for the employee with the given id
sessFact.evictCollection("Empl.contactNos"); //evict all "contactNo" collections
```

89: How can hibernate sessionfactory be bound to JNDI?

Answer:

We can hibernate sessionfactory be bound to JNDI by using "hibernate.jndi.url" and "hibernate.jndi.class" properties in hibernate configuration file to instantiate an initial context.

```
<property name=" hibernate.session_factory_name ">
    java:jdbc/HibernateSessionFactory
</property>
```

Chapter 9

Hibernate Interceptor and Filters

90: What is an EmptyInterceptor? How is it used in Hibernate?

Answer:

Interceptors in Hibernate allows various lifecycle events to be handled in a specific way. For example, if you want the application to do something upon creation of a new customer record in the database, you can use the Interceptor methods and implement it according to your requirement. An EmptyInterceptor is a framework or an interface that provides the necessary methods to handle the particular lifecycle event. The EmptyInterceptor brings with it more than 9 important lifecycle events that you can handle appropriately to bring in your business logic. It can be considered as the base interceptor to be implemented for handling database events.

91: What is the difference between Interceptors and Filters?

Answer:

Even though the Interceptors and Filters are based on intercepting filters, their methods, scope and functionality differ considerably. While a filter is used only with Servlet specifications, the Interceptors can be used anywhere. Filters do not have configurable method calls, whereas the interceptor methods can be configured whether or not to be executed with includemethods or excludemethods. Filters work only with the URLs for which they are created while Interceptors work for a lot of lifecycle events whenever they happen. While the interceptors work more with the business logic, the filters work more with the deployment configurations.

92: How will you execute certain logic on every execution of CRUD operation of session, without having code duplication?

Answer:

We can execute certain logic on every execution of CRUD operation of session, without having code duplication by:

a) Using Hibernate Interceptors such as Session level and SessionFactory level interceptors
b) Used to execute certain logic such as updating "AuditLog" table for each CRUD operations

93: What is the use of Hibernate Filter?

Answer:

Hibernate filter is:

a) Used to filter data retrieved from the database

b) Has global access, unique name, parameterized value (in filter-param tag>)

c) Can be enabled or disabled

94: Where will you define Filter and how?

Answer:

Filter is defined:

a) Using <filter-def> tag

b) Invoke the filter within class mapping in hibernate configuration file

c) For instance, if filter parameter is set to 60, the query will retrieve the user details whose age is greater than or equal to (>=) 60

```
<class name=".." table="..." >
    ...
    <filter name="userFilter" condition="age >= :
    userFilterParameter" />
</class>
<filter-def name="userFilter">
    <filter-param name="userFilterParameter"
    type="Integer" />
</filter-def>
```

95: How will you enable or disable hibernate Filter?

Answer:

a) To enable the filter.

```
Filter myfilter = sessn.enableFilter ("userFilter");
myfilter.setParameter ("userFilterParameter", new
Integer(60) );
```

b) To disable the filter.

```
sessn.disableFilter("userFilter ");
```

Spring

This page is intentionally left blank.

Chapter **10**

Spring Modules

96: What are the modules available in Spring Core Container Module?

Answer:

The Spring Core Container Module is responsible for some of the most important features of Spring. It contains the Core, Context, Beans, and Expression Language modules. The core and the beans modules are responsible for the most important features of spring that are Inversion of Control or IoC and Dependency Injection. The Context module takes care of Internationalization, Event propagation, EJB, resource loading, JMX, and basic remoting. The Expression Language module or the EL module is an extension of the EL in JSP. Important features such as method invocation, getting and setting property values, accessing objects, collections, variables and indexers, and arithmetic and logical operators are a part of the EL module.

97: What are the modules available in Spring Data Access / Integration Module?

Answer:

As the name suggests, the Data Access / Integration module contains the important modules and features related to database, relations, and transactions. This further comprises of the Java DataBase Connectivity, Object XML Mappers, Object Relational Mapping, Java Message Service and Transaction modules. Database connections are maintained easily with the JDBC that acts as a transparent layer managing the vendor specific coding for the particular database. ORM module manages the Object Relational Mapping which consists of Hibernate, JDO, JPA etc. OXM handles the Object – XML Mapping which facilitates writing into and reading from XML beans and XStream. JMS is responsible for all messaging requirements, incoming and outgoing. Transaction facilitates transaction programming using special interfaces and POJO.

98: What are the modules available in Spring Web Module?

Answer:

The Web layer consists of the Web, Portlet, Servlet and Struts which facilitate web applications. The Web module handles the servlet listeners and a web-based application context. It also extends the basic remoting aspects of web applications. The Servlet module is responsible for the Spring MVC implementation of the web application. It helps better integration with the rest of the Spring framework. The Portlet is similar to the Servlet module. It basically mirrors the Servlet module features to function in a

Portlet environment. The Web-Struts integrates the Spring with the classic struts web tier. Together, these modules support a web application.

99: What are the modules in Spring Framework?

Answer:

The various modules in Spring Framework are:

a) Core module (IoC container)
b) AOP module (Aspect Oriented Programming)
c) DAO module (Spring DAO support, JDBC support, transaction management)
d) ORM module (Object/Relational mapping - Integration with Hibernate, iBatis, JPA)
e) Spring MVC (JSP)
f) Spring Context module (Application context, JNDI support, Remoting support)
g) Spring Web module (Web Application context, Integration with Struts)

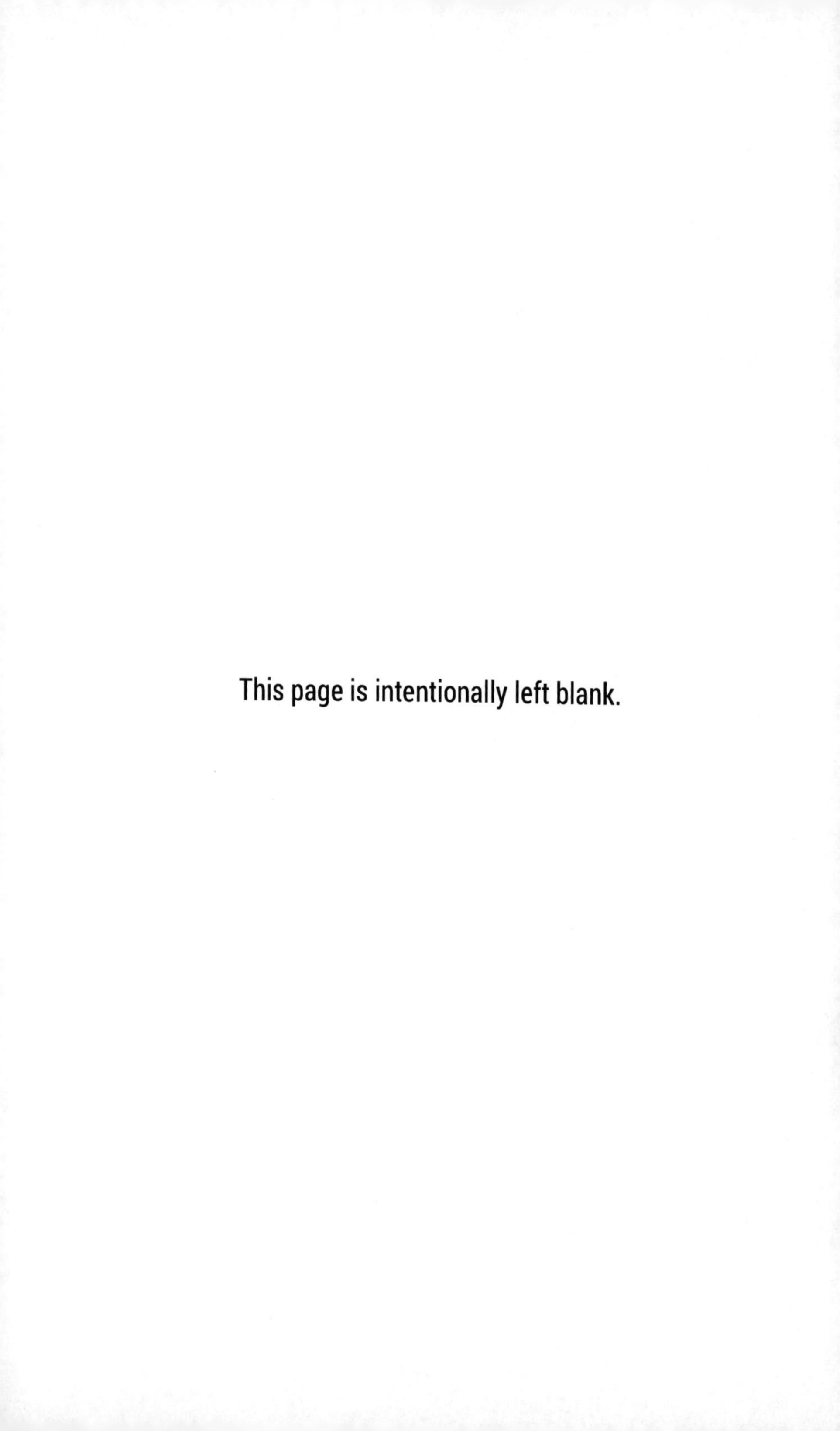

This page is intentionally left blank.

Chapter **11**

IoC Container

100: Explain the 2 types of IoC containers.

Answer:

The IoC container consists of the BeanFactory and ApplicationContext containers. The BeanFactory interface is capable of maintaining different resource registries and their dependencies. It enables you to read the bean definitions and create them as per the XML that contains the definition. But first you need to create a FileInputStream, FileSystemResource, ClassPathResource, or a ClassPathXmlApplicationContext which contains the Bean definition and then use a XmlBeanFactory to create a BeanFactory. The ApplicationContext container takes care of the text messages and event listeners that make the applications function according to the business logic. The ApplicationContext can overtake the BeanFactory since it contains all the functionality of the BeanFactory. Ideally, the Beanfactory is preferred when we have a lighter application such as a mobile app or an Applet.

101: Which is a better practice to follow – constructor based or setter based DI?

Answer:

Springs support injecting bean dependency via constructors and setters. Both have their own pros and cons. Here's the list of the differences and why one should be chosen over the other.

a) The first and the obvious difference is the way the dependency is injected. It is done either using the constructors or using the setXXX () or setter function.
b) When using the constructor, as soon as the object instance is created, the dependency is injected. It is more implicit in nature. When using the setter methods, dependency injection is explicit and more readable.
c) While the setter injection can be overridden as it can be called any number of times, the constructor injection cannot be applied more than once on one object as every time you call the constructor, a new object will be created.
d) When using a constructor, the dependency is assured whereas in setter injection, it is not assured till the setter function is explicitly invoked.
e) When the objects have circular dependency, the setter injection is better as otherwise ObjectCurrentlyInCreationException may be thrown.

102: What is meant by IoC and DI?

Answer:

a) IoC (Inversion of Control) is a principal that is implemented by using DI (Dependency Injection) design pattern
b) It is used to reduce tight coupling between components which is done through programs and separate the same in configuration file. Tight coupling means that the dependencies of components will be hardcoded in the program
c) Example of IoC container: BeanFactory and ApplicationContext
d) BeanFactory and ApplicationContext interfaces are the representation of Spring IoC container
e) ApplicationContext is the subclass of BeanFactory and XmlBeanFactory is the most commonly used implementation of BeanFactory

103: What is the use of Spring Container?

Answer:

The uses of Spring Container are as follows:

a) Used to instantiate and manage the beans
b) Used to maintain the required dependencies between the objects through the spring configuration file

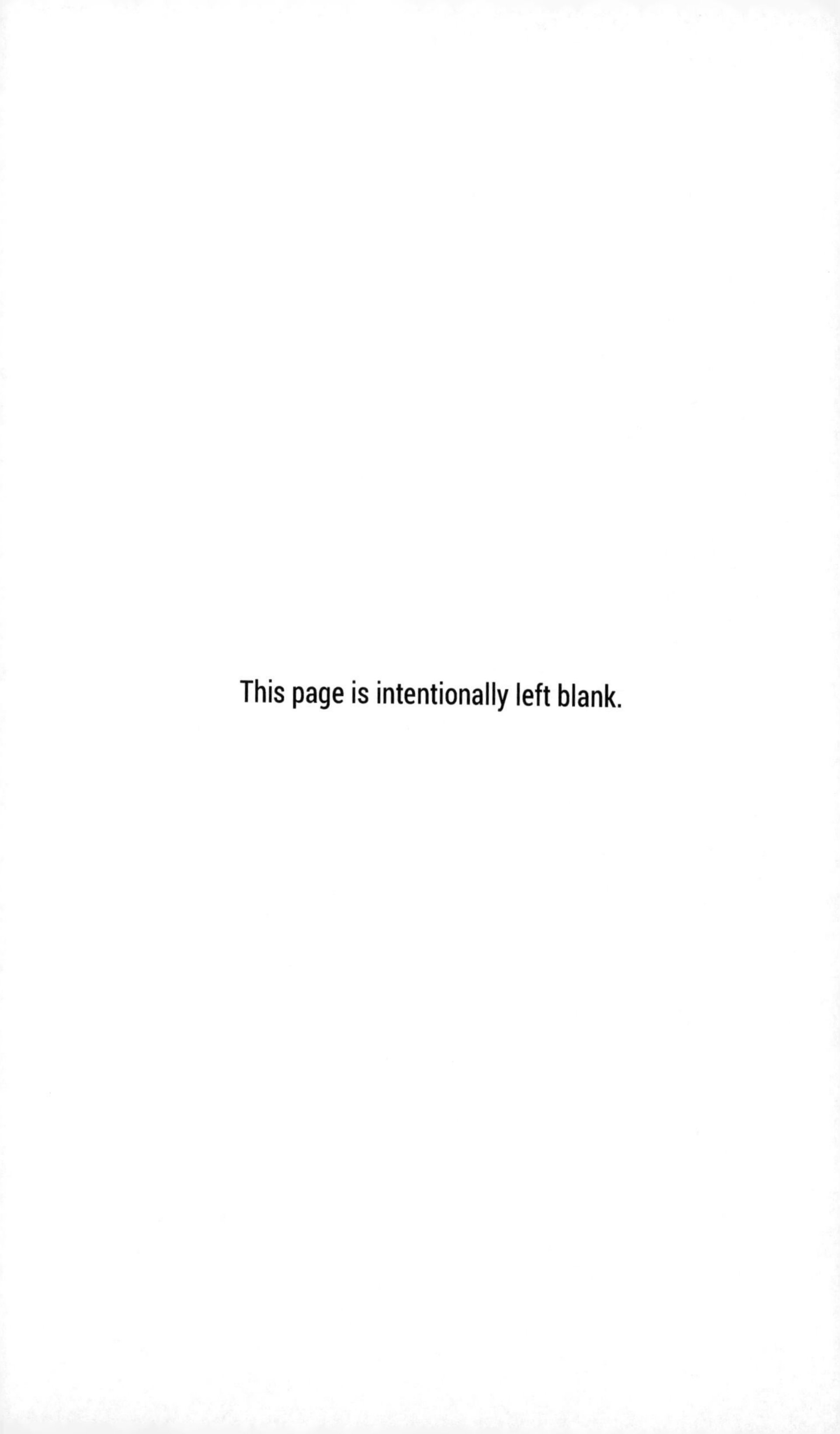
This page is intentionally left blank.

Chapter **12**

Beans

104: Explain the Lifecycle of a Spring Bean.

Answer:

The 2 major stages of a Spring Bean's lifecycle are its initialization and destruction. You can define the bean properties in an XML file, using Annotations or using Plain Old Java code. You can create Spring Beans outside the Spring container and yet access it in the ApplicationContext. Basically, the lifecycle events of the bean can be categorized as post-initialization and pre-destruction. Once the basic bean properties are set in XML or through Annotations, the InitializingBean interface initializes the bean. The DisposableBean interface makes sure that the bean gets a callback when its container is destroyed. The various Aware Interfaces will let you inject specific dependencies and behaviour. The custom init() method initializes the bean and destroy() method destroys the bean when it is no longer needed. You can use the

@PostConstruct to do specific job just when the bean has been created and not yet returned to the object instance. You can use the @PreDestroy annotation to include any business logic just before the bean is destroyed.

105: What is meant by Beans in Spring?

Answer:

a) Beans are the objects that are instantiated and managed by the Spring IoC Container.
b) Beans dependencies are configured in spring configuration xml file that is used by the container.

106: How would you instantiate the container?

Answer:

We can instantiate a container using FileSystemResource, ClassPathResource and ClassPathXmlApplicationContext.

a) **BeanFactory:**

   Resource resrc = new FileSystemResource("spring-beans.xml");

   BeanFactory bf = new XmlBeanFactory (resrc);

   ClassPathResource cpresrc = new ClassPathResource("spring-beans.xml");

   BeanFactory bf = new XmlBeanFactory (cpresrc);

b) **ApplicationContext:**

   ApplicationContext actxt = new ClassPathXmlApplicationContext (new String [] {"spring-beans1.xml", "/com/ks/java/spring-beans2.xml"});

   BeanFactory bf = (BeanFactory) actxt;

107: What is the difference between bean id and name attribute?

Answer:

The differences between bean id and name attribute are as below:

a) **Id:**
   i) Unique identifier
   ii) Not accept special character such as "/", "*" which are used in URL
   iii) If duplicate id is given, it XML parser will throw compilation error
   iv) Id and name attributes are not required for inner bean as it will be ignored by the container

b) **Name:**
   i) Not unique
   ii) Used to give URL name that contains "/" in Spring MVC
   iii) If bean name attribute is not given explicitly, the container will generate a unique name for the bean

108: How will you achieve Factory design pattern in spring for Bean Creation?

Answer:

Bean can be created via Static Factory Method and Instance (non-static) Factory Method.

a) **Static Factory Method:**
   i) Use "factory-method" attribute of bean tag (factory bean creation)
   ii) Call static factory method defined in Bean Factory class

iii) <bean id="id1" class="com.factory.beanFactory" factory-method="factmtd1" />

b) **Instance Factory Method:**

i) Use "factory-method" and "factory-bean" attributes

ii) Call instance method of Bean Factory class using its bean

iii) <bean id="factBean" class="com.factory.beanFactory" />

iv) <bean id="catBean" factory-bean="factBean" factory-method="factmtd1" />

Chapter **13**

Dependency Injection

109: Explain Dependency Injection by Setter method.

Answer:

Dependency Injection by Setter method can be done in 3 ways –

a) **Injecting Strings and other Primitive values**

Here, we are creating different Setter methods for setting the value of different member variables. For example, if you have Student entity with StudentId, StudentName and ClassId, setStudentId(int studid), setStudentName(String studname) and setClassId(int classid) methods are defined each of which would accept the corresponding primitive or string data type and set the member value of the current object with *this* operator.

b) **Injecting a Dependent Object**

Here, the reference of a new bean is created using the ref attribute of the property element. It is similar to declaring an object as the data member of another object. Whenever the main object is instantiated, the dependent object is also instantiated. For Example,

```
<bean id="myAddress" class=<class_path>>
<property name="myAddLine1" value="15G, Whispering Palms"></property>
<property name="myCity" value="Mumbai"></property>
<property name="myState"
value="Maharashtra"></property>
<property name="myCountry" value="India"></property>
</bean>
<bean id="myPerson" class=<class_path>>
<property name="perId" value="23"></property>
<property name="perName" value="Sridevi Srinivas"></property>
<property name="myAdd" ref="myAddress"></property>
</bean>
```

c) **Injecting Collections**

Here, you declare one of the elements as a collection such as a list, set or map. This is referred in the ApplicationContext as below:

```
<bean id="myStudent" class=<class_path>>
<property name="studId" value="45"></property>
<property name="StudName" value="Sridevi Srinivas"></property>
<property name="PercentageMarks">
<list>
<value>Term 1 80%</value>
<value> Term 2 85%</value>
```

```
<value> Term 3 82%</value>
</list>
</property>
</bean>
```

110: What are the types of Dependency Injections in Spring?

Answer:

The types of Dependency Injections in Spring are:

a) **Constructor Injection:** <constructor-arg >
b) **Setter Injection:** <property name="animal">

111: How will you inject a bean into another bean via Constructor injection?

Answer:

We can inject a bean into another bean via Constructor injection as below:

```
<bean id="bean1" class="..." />
<bean id="bean2" class="...">
    <constructor-arg ref="bean1" />
</bean>
```

112: How will you assign values to the constructor primitive type arguments?

Answer:

We can assign values to the constructor primitive type arguments as below:

```
<bean id="..." class="..." >
    <constructor-arg type="String" value="abc" />
```

```
    <constructor-arg type="int" value="10" />
</bean>
```

113: How will you assign values to the constructor arguments if it contains 2 arguments of the same type?

Answer:

We can assign values to the constructor arguments if it contains 2 arguments of the same type as below:

```
<bean id="animal" class="...">
    <constructor-arg type="String" value="cat" index="0" />
    <constructor-arg type="String" value="dog" index="1" />
</bean>
```

Chapter **14**

Importing XML Resource

114: How can you load an external resource file into the spring context?

Answer:

You can load an external resource file into a spring resource object and get the file input stream for the same. You can enter the resource path which could be a text file, xml file, a classpath or even a url. A custom loader bean is created first, the given class path is checked and package file is loaded. While the basic file reading is done by a BufferedReader, the ResourceLoader actually loads the file from the mentioned path or URL. Alternatively, you can import using the import tag as

<import resource = "Classpath*:/<_resource_filename_> />

The classpath* indicates a search in the entire classpath without restricting in one path. The _resource_filename_ is the xml file from which data or properties have to be imported. You can

include multiple resources this way, one after the other.
Or else, you can include a resource file using the ApplicationContext using

```
ApplicationContext myAppContext =
new ClassPathXmlApplicationContext (<_resource_filename_>);
```

115: How do you make the resource file name configurable?

Answer:

To make the resource file name configurable, you can include it in the ApplicationContext as below:

```
<bean id="configurableResourceLoader" class =
"<package.class>">
    <property name = "resource">
        <value>classpath:myClasspathResource.xml</value>
    </property>
</bean>
```

The value tag can contain a URL, classpath, or a filepath instead of myClasspathResource.xml. It could be a text file, or an xml file. Once this resource is set, the value for the resource can be easily configured in the ApplicationContext.

116: How will you access the beans defined in other xml configuration files?

Answer:

We can access the beans defined in other xml configuration files by importing all the required xml files into the mail configuration file.

Spring-bean3.xml:

```
<import resource="spring-bean1.xml" />
<import resource="dir2/spring-bean2.xml" />
<bean id="..." class="..." />
```

117: How will you import the constants given in the properties file into the XML configuration file?

Answer:

We can import the constants given in the properties file into the XML configuration file by giving the relative path of properties file in the "location" attribute of <context:property-placeholder> tag.

```
    <context:property-placeholder
    location="/ApplProperties.properties" />
```

118: How will you use the constants defined in the properties file instead of XML file?

Answer:

We can use the constants defined in the properties file instead of XML file as below:

```
<context:property-placeholder
location="/ApplProperties.properties" />
<bean id="..." class="....">
    <property name="dbname" value="$ { appl.dbname }" />
</bean>
```

This page is intentionally left blank.

Chapter **15**

Idref Element

119: Explain the following code snippet. How do you make it work?

```
package com.mySpringTrial.spring;
public class myShape {
    private myPoint myPointA;
        //Define the Getters and Setters for myPointA
}
    package com.mySpringTrial.spring;
    public class myPoint {
        private int pointAB;
        private int pointBC;
        public int getValueOfA() {
        return pointAB;
    }
    public void setValueOfA(int valueOfA) {
```

```
        pointAB = valueOfA;
    }
    public int getValueOfB() {
        return pointBC;
    }
    public void setValueOfB(int valueOfB) {
        pointBC = valueOfA;
    }
}
```

The Spring configuration file comes as follows:

```
<bean id=" myShape"
class="com.mySpringTrial.spring.myShape">
<property name="myPointA">
<idref bean="myShapePointA"/>
</property>
</bean>
<bean id=" myShapePointA"
class="com.mySpringTrial.spring.myPoint">
<property name="pointAB" value="45"></property>
<property name="pointBC" value="60"></property>
</bean>
```

Answer:

This code will not work as the idref expects a string. Here we are trying to pass an object of type myPoint instead (since myShapePointA is of type com.mySpringTrial.spring.myPoint).
To make it work, you can use the ref instead of IDRef and include a String type in the myShape Bean. So the above code changes into

```
public class myShape {
    private myPoint myPointA;
```

```
    private String myPointName;
        //Define the Getters and Setters for pointA
}
<bean id=" myShape"
class="com.mySpringTrial.spring.myShape">
<property name="myPointA">
<ref bean="myShapePointA"/>
</property>
<property name=" myPointName ">
<idref bean="myShapePointA"/>
</property>
</bean>
```

120: What is the advantage of using an IdRef instead of value?

Answer:

When using the idref tag instead of value, the XML Parser will validate the existence of the bean. When using the value tag, the bean existence is not checked by the Parser and it will end up throwing an exception or error. Even though the idref id has to start with a letter followed by letters, numbers and some of the allowed special characters, it rarely creates a constraint issue. Though you can create a Bean using simple Java Code, creating one using XML makes it persistent and configurable. Then you can use the XML parser to extract or include the details in your program. Using the idref implies the validation of the bean's existence.

121: What is the difference between ref and idref attributes in spring?

Answer:

Both are used to inject a bean into another bean via <constructor-arg> or <property> tags.

a) **Ref:** Have the value of "id" or "name" of the another bean
b) **Idref:** Have only the id of another bean

122: Write down an example of ref and idref.

Answer:

a) **Ref:**

```
<bean name="bean1" class="..."/>
<bean id="bean2" class="...">
    <property name="animal" ref="bean1"/>
</bean>
```

b) **Idref:**

```
<bean id="bean1" class="..."/>
<bean id="bean2" class="...">
    <property name="animal">
        <idref bean="bean1"/>
    </property>
</bean>
```

123: Write down an example using <value> and <idref>.

Answer:

a)
```
<bean id="bean1" class="..." />
<bean id="bean2" class="...">
    <property name="animal" value="bean1"/>
</bean>
```

b)
```
<bean id="bean1" class="..." />
```

```
<bean id="bean2" class="...">
    <property name="animal" idref="bean1"/>
</bean>
```

124: What will happen if you use "value" attribute instead of <idref> while injecting a bean using <property> tag?

Answer:

a) **Idref:** Container validates the bean at the deployment time whether the referenced bean exists
b) **Value:** No validation is done on the referenced bean

This page is intentionally left blank.

Chapter **16**

Bean Collaborators

125: What are Bean Collaborators?

Answer:

Bean Collaborators are a reference to a bean. When you reference a bean from within another bean, the bean collaborators come in action. The <ref> tag is used to set a reference to another bean from within a bean tag. Within the <constructor-arg> tag, the <ref> tag is used to reference a bean. If the referencing bean is also defined in the same ApplicationContext file, the bean name is specified in the local attribute of ref tag. For example, <ref local = "myStudents"/>. If the referencing bean is defined in another ApplicationContext file, it is referenced with the bean attribute. For example, <ref bean = "myStudents"/>

126: Can I reference a bean defined in the parent container of the current bean? Explain.

Answer:

Yes, a bean can reference the parent container bean using the parent attribute of the <ref> tag. Set the value of the *parent* attribute to the *id* of the parent bean to make this effective. If the parent bean is defined as <bean id = "myParentBean" class = "class_path"> </bean>, then the bean trying to reference this parent bean must have the following *ref* tag.

```
<bean id = "myParentBean" class = "class_path">
    <property name = "target">
        <ref parent = "myParentBean"/>
    </property>
</bean>
```

This is mainly used when you have to wrap a chain of beans using a proxy of the existing parent bean.

127: What are the advantages of using bean collaborators?

Answer:

Bean references are explicitly set via the collaborators. While there are many ways to set the reference, they all provide documentation for all the references set in the program for the beans. If there is no reference set explicitly, another implicit process called autowiring will take over and set the necessary references. But when the beans are *autowired,* it becomes very difficult to determine the references for each bean. Moreover, autowiring in itself is confusing as it can be overridden in different ways at different levels. Hence, setting the references explicitly is considered the best practice and bean collaborators help the programmer set references explicitly.

128: What is the difference between "local" and "bean" attribute of <ref> tag?

Answer:

a) **<ref bean="bean1" /> :**
   i) The attribute "bean" value may be same as "id" attribute or one of the "name" attribute of some other/referenced bean
   ii) The bean reference to any bean can be created in the same container or its parent container regardless of whether the bean is in the same XML file or not

b) **<ref local="bean1" /> :**
   i) The attribute "bean" value should be same as "id" attribute of some other/referenced bean
   ii) The bean definition should be present within the same XML file. If it is not, the XML parser will throw an error

129: Explain about "parent" attribute of <ref> tag.

Answer:

a) <ref parent ="bean1" />
b) The value of parent attribute can have "id" or "name" attribute value of referenced bean
c) The target/referenced bean should be in the parent container (BeanFactory/ApplicationContext) of the current one
d) It is used when the existing bean needs to be wrapped with some proxy bean that will have the same name as the parent bean

e) <bean id="bean1" class="..." />

<bean id="bean2" class="org.springframework.aop.framework.ProxyFactoryBean" >

<property name="target" ref="bean1" />

(OR)

<property name="target">

<ref parent="bean1">

</property>

</bean>

Chapter **17**

Collections

130: Explain the code for using a List collection in Spring.

Answer:

Consider a Tourist class with a list of locations the tourist has visited. Given below is a code snippet of how to declare the class and how to add the List values.

```
public class myTouristClass {
    private String touristName;
    private int touristMobile;
    private List<object> myTourDestinations;
    // Further implementations
}
```

In the ApplicationContext file the following tags have to be included.

```
<ref bean="myTouristClass " />
```

```
<bean class="class_path">
    <property name="touristName" value="Tourist1" />
    <property name=" touristMobile" value="6372519831" />
</bean>
<property name="myTourDestinations">
    <list>
        <value>India</value>
        <value>Spain</value>
        <value> Africa</value>
        <value>USA</value>
    </list>
</property>
```

131: Explain the code for using a Map collection in Spring.

Answer:

Consider a Tourist class with a set of locations the tourist has visited. Given below is a code snippet of how to declare the class and how to add the Set values.

```
public class myTouristClass {
    private String touristName;
    private int touristMobile;
    private Set<object> myTourDestinations;
    // Further implementations
}
```

In the ApplicationContext file the following tags have to be included.

```
<ref bean="myTouristClass " />
```

```
<bean class="class_path">
    <property name="touristName" value="Tourist1" />
    <property name=" touristMobile" value="6372519831" />
</bean>
<property name="myTourDestinations">
    <set>
        <value>India</value>
        <value>Spain</value>
        <value> Africa</value>
        <value>USA</value>
    </set>
</property>
```

132: Explain the code for using a Properties collection in Spring.

Answer:

Consider a Tourist class with a collection of locations and the order the tourist has visited. Given below is a code snippet of how to declare the class and how to add a collection or property values.

```
public class myTouristClass {
    private String touristName;
    private int touristMobile;
    private Properties<object, object> myTourDestinations;
    // Further implementations
}
```

In the ApplicationContext file the following tags have to be included.

```
<ref bean="myTouristClass " />
```

```
<bean class="class_path">
    <property name="touristName" value="Tourist1" />
    <property name=" touristMobile" value="6372519831" />
</bean>
<property name="myTourDestinations">
    <props>
        <prop key= "First">India</value>
        < prop key= "Second">Spain</value>
        < prop key= "Third">Africa</value>
        < prop key= "Fourth">USA</value>
    </props>
</property>
```

133: What are the types of collections that are supported by Spring?

Answer:

The types of collections that are supported by Spring are List, Map, Set and Props are supported by using the following elements within <property name="..."> tag.

a) <list>, <value> or <ref bean="" />, </map>
b) <set>, <value> or <ref bean="" />, </set>
c) <map>, <entry key="... " value="..." />, </map>
d) <props>, <prop key="..." value="..." />, </props>

134: How will you append the parent class properties with the child properties?

Answer:

We can append the parent class properties with the child

properties by using "merge" attribute in the child properties definition.

```
<bean id="animal" class="...">
    <property name="emails">
        <list>
            <value> email1 </value>
            <value> email2</value>
        </list>
    </property>
<bean>
<bean id="cat" class="..."   parent="animal" >
    <property name="emails">
        <list merge="true">
            <value> email1 </value>
            <value> email2</value>
        </list>
    </property>
<bean>
```

135: How will you assign "null" and " " empty string to the bean arguments?

Answer:

a)
```
<bean id="..." class="...">
    <property name="uname" value="" />
</bean>
```

b)
```
<bean id="..." class="...">
    <property name="uname"> <null/> </property>
</bean>
```

This page is intentionally left blank.

Chapter **18**

Depends-on Attribute

136: What is the Depends-on Attribute used for?

Answer:

The Depends-On attribute of *bean* tag is used to explicitly list out the beans that the current bean is dependent on so that those beans will be loaded before creating the current bean. For example, if an Order bean is dependent on Customer, Category and Item beans, these 3 beans are listed in the Depends-On attribute so that they are loaded before the Order bean is created. It basically establishes the dependency of the beans and makes sure that the dependent beans are available when a bean is created. The format is as follows:

<bean id = "myOrder" class = "<classpath>" depends-on= "myCustomer, myCategory, myItem/>

<bean id = "myCustomer" class = "<classpath>" />

<bean id = "myCategory" class = "<classpath>" />

```
<bean id = "myItem" class = "<classpath>" />
```

137: Can you add a bean that depends on a singleton bean? Explain.

Answer:

Yes. It is possible to inject dependency on singleton beans. You can do this by making the scope prototype or proxy.

```
<bean id="myBean1" class = "<class_type>">
    <property name="myBean2" ref="myBean2"/>
</bean>
<bean id="myBean2" scope="prototype" class = "<class_type>"/>
```

Even if you try to initiate the ApplicationContext multiple times, it will not create a new myBean1 instance since it is a singleton bean. When the ApplicationContext is initialized the first time, an instance of myBean1 is created and the same is used for further requests. This can be taken care of in 2 ways – by Lookup Injection method or by Scoped Proxies. In the Lookup Injection Method, the getter method for the singleton bean is called every time the ApplicationContext is approached. When using scoped-proxies, a proxy is created for the prototype bean instead of the singleton bean.

138: Write a simple example using depends-on attribute.

Answer:

We need to create different class files, XML file which has the bean configuration and the main file.

Code for myFirstBean.java

```
package com.myTrialPackage;
```

```
public class myFirstBean {
    public myFirstBean() {
        System.out.println("Class my First Bean is initialized");
    }
}
```

Code for mySecondBean.java

```
package com.myTrialPackage;
public class mySecondBean {
    public mySecondBean() {
        System.out.println("Class my Second Bean Initialized");
    }
}
```

Save the following code in spring-depends-on.xml which is the bean configuration file

You have to include the standard xml schema for beans and util using the beans tag first and then include the following bean element.

```
<bean id = "myFirstBean" class =
"com.myTrialPackage.myFirstBean" depends-on =
"mySecondBean"/>
<bean id = "mySecondBean" class =
"com.myTrialPackage.mySecondBean"/>
</beans>
```

Save this as mySpringDependsTest.java. This contains the main function.

```
package com.myTrialPackage;
import org.springframework.context.ApplicationContext;
import
org.springframework.context.support.ClassPathXmlApplicationC
ontext;
```

```
public class mySpringDependsTest {
    public static void main(String[] myArgs) {
        ApplicationContext myContext =
            new ClassPathXmlApplicationContext ("spring-
            depends-on.xml");

    }
}
```

When you run mySpringDependsTest program, the output will be:

Class my Second Bean Initialized

Class my First Bean Initialized

139: How will you specify the bean dependency explicitly?

Answer:

The attribute "depends-on" needs to be specified in <bean> tag. If any other beans needs to be initialized before the current/particular bean is initialized, depends-on attribute can be given. For instance, before doing database operations, database driver needs to be registered.

```
<bean id="bean1" class="..." depends-on="bean2" />
<bean id="bean2Dao" class="..." />
```

140: Which bean will be destroyed first if "depends-on" attribute is used to define bean dependencies?

Answer:

Dependent beans will be destroyed first as initialization time prior to the bean where depends-on attribute is given.

Chapter **19**

Lazy Initialized Bean

141: What is the advantage of Lazy initialization?

Answer:

Generally, the ApplicationContext creates an instance of all singleton beans in the application startup itself. Even though this is a good strategy to validate the bean configuration in the early stages itself, it tends to make the starting up very slow. Moreover, more memory is unnecessarily help up for the initialized classes. Instead, if the *lazy-init* mode is set to *true* in bean configuration, it is initiated only when the bean is requested by the application. The *lazy-init* can be set to true, false or default. By default, it is false. You can change the default value in the ApplicationContext for *lazy-init-default*.

142: Analyze the following piece of code from a bean configuration. Explain how it affects the initialization of the

bean.

<bean id = "myDearBean" class = "<class_path>" lazy-init = "default"/>

Answer:

The *lazy-init* attribute, when set to default, takes the value of *lazy-init-default* which can be set to true or false at the Application level. By default, the value of *lazy-init-default* is *false* and hence, the value of *lazy-init* will be set to *false*. If the value of *lazy-init-default* is set to *true* explicitly, then the value of *lazy-init* will be set to the same. By default, the value of *lazy-init* is *false.*

143: How will you prevent the pre-instantiation of a singleton bean?

Answer:

a) We can prevent the pre-instantiation of a singleton bean by using the attribute "lazy-init" in <bean> tag
b) IoC container instantiates this bean when it is first requested meaning that Container creates an instance for this bean when it is first requested rather than creating when the ApplicationContext is starting up
c) <bean id="bean1" class="..." lazy-init="true" />

144: How will you handle the singleton bean which depends on a lazy initialized bean?

Answer:

a) We can handle the singleton bean which depends on a lazy initialized bean by using "default-lazy-init" attribute in <bean> tag

b) When the singleton bean depends on lazy initialized bean, container will create a bean instance for lazy initialized bean at startup. Otherwise it will not satisfy singleton bean's dependency and it will not be injected into the singleton bean

c) <bean id="bean1" class="..." default-lazy-init="true" />

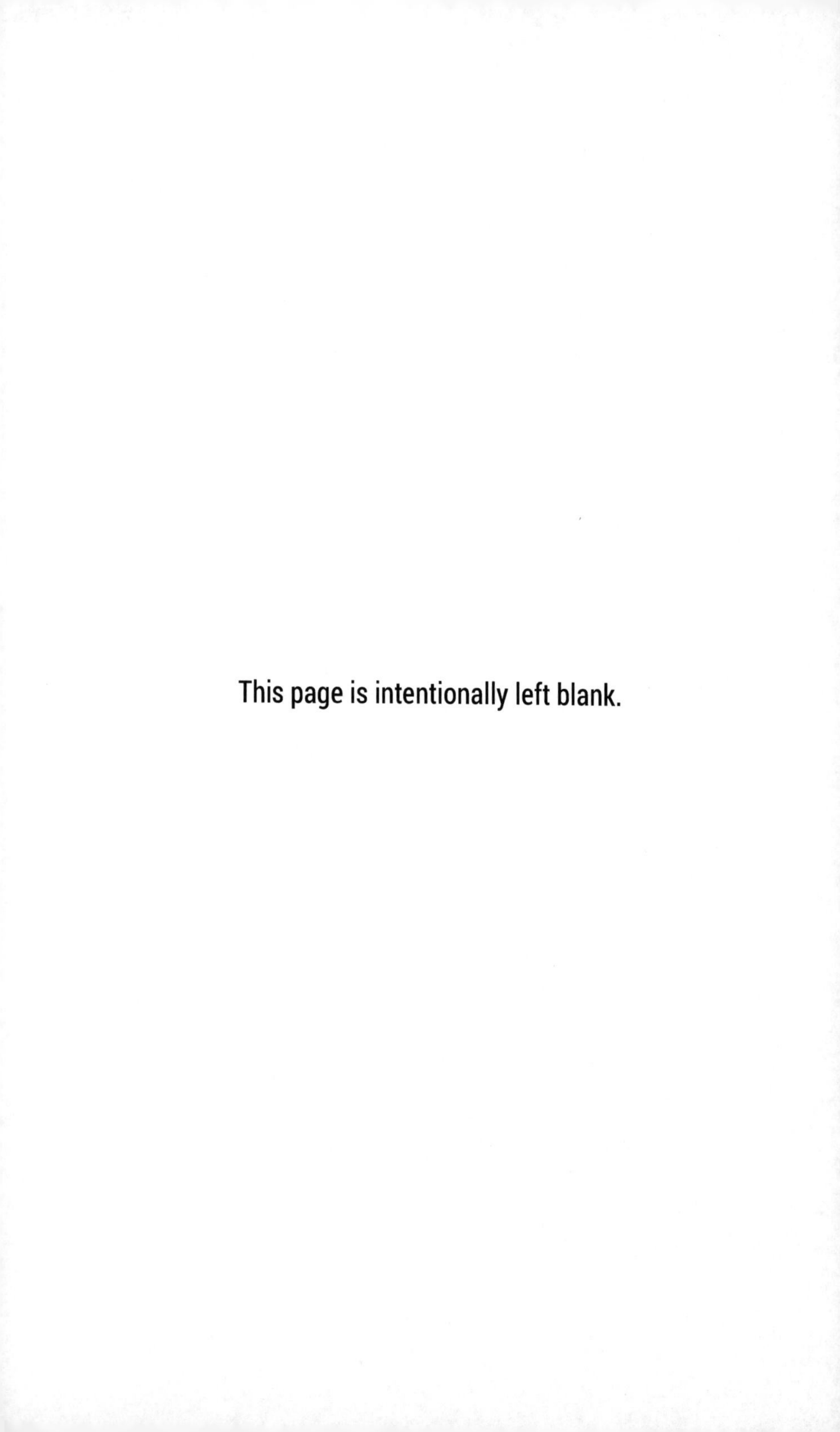
This page is intentionally left blank.

Chapter **20**

Autowiring

145: How do you make autowiring error-safe?

Answer:

Autowiring is the process by which your bean collaborators are automatically set and reference a bean based on the BeanFactory. It is bean specific, that is, one bean can be autowired while another not. To make autowiring error-safe, the *required* attribute of *@Autowired* annotation is set to *false*. You can then set the *autowire* or *autowire-candidate* to *true* or *false* for specific beans in the ApplicationContext or bean configuration xml to include or exclude specific beans from autowiring irrespective of the *@Autowired* annotation value set. The *autowire* attribute must to set to *constructor* and *autowire-candidate* to *false* if a bean has to be explicitly made not available for autowiring and to make it error-safe.

146: What are the limitations of autowiring?

Answer:

Even though autowiring automates the referencing part of required beans, it has some limitations too which programmers need to consider. The first and most obvious issue is that the property can be overridden in many ways. Since autowiring can be set for each bean, even if you have set *@Autowired (required = false)* it is quite possible that 90% of your beans have set their autowiring to *true* and vice-versa. When not set explicitly, the status of autowiring for a bean is confusing. Hence, explicit wiring is recommended over autowiring. You can set the dependencies in many other ways using the *<property>* or the *<constructor-arg>*. These options will definitely override the autowiring settings. Another issue with autowiring is that, it is not possible with primitive data types, classes and strings.

147: What is meant by Autowiring in Spring and what is its advantage?

Answer:

a) Spring Container autowires/creates relationship between collaborating beans
b) The main advantage of autowire is that it reduces the need to specify property and constructor arguments in the XML file
c) The dependencies being set explicitly using property and constructor injection overrides Autowiring
d) E.g. <bean id=".." class=".." autowire="byname" />

148: What are the different modes/types of Autowiring?

Answer:

Five modes:

a) **No:** Default and no autowire

b) **byname:**

   i) Autowire by property name

   ii) If a bean contains a property that needs to be autowired and it defines autowire="byname", container will look for other bean which has same name as the property name of the autowired bean

c) **byType:**

   i) Autowire by data type of the property name

   ii) Container will check whether there is exactly one bean exists with this property name. If so, it would autowire the bean with the property name which is of same data type with the bean

   iii) If more than one bean contains the same name as property name, fatal error will be thrown

   iv) Autowire via setter method

d) **Constructor:**

   i) Autowire by the data type of the constructor arguments

   ii) Container autowires if the datatype of the bean is same as the datatype of the constructor arguments

   iii) If more than one bean contains the same datatype as constructor arguments, fatal error will be thrown

   iv) Autowire via constructor

e) **autodetect:**

i) Autowire by "byType" or "constructor"
ii) If default constructor is found, Container will use "constructor" type otherwise use "byType"

149: How will you prevent a bean from Autowiring?

Answer:

We can prevent a bean from Autowiring by setting "autowire-candidate" attribute in <bean> tag to "false". To exclude beans from Autowiring based on pattern matching, use "default-autowire-candidates" attribute.

Chapter **21**

Bean Scopes

150: Which are the bean scopes available with web applications?

Answer:

The bean scopes available with web applications are session, request and global-session. The bean scopes basically define the availability or the accessibility of the bean through the application. When the scope is no longer valid, the bean is no longer available. These scopes are available only in a web-aware implementation of the application context. When the *scope* of a bean is set to *request,* for every HTTP request, an instance of the bean will be created. When the *scope* of a bean is set to *session,* for every HTTP session, an instance of the bean will be created. When the *scope* of a bean is set to *globalSession,* the bean is globally available throughout the global portlet session.

151: How do you set the bean scope using Annotations?

Answer:

To set the bean scope, you can either use the XML tags or use the Annotations. When using the @Scope annotation, you can do it in 2 ways:

a) @Scope ("<bean_scope>"), where bean_scope can be singleton or prototype

   @Scope (ConfigurableBeanFactory.SCOPE_Prototype) or @Scope(ConfigurableBeanFactory.SCOPE_Singleton)

   @Scope (value = "<bean_scope>" proxyMode = ScopedProxyMode.TARGET_CLASS), where bean_scope can be request, session or globalSession.

   @Scope (value = "application" proxyMode = ScopedProxyMode.TARGET_CLASS). With @Scope, you can set the bean scope to Application also.

152: How do you create custom scopes?

Answer:

Spring 2.0 onwards allows creation and implementation of custom scopes. You can either create a new scope from the scratch or use it to enhance an existing scope. The latter option is available only with the web-scopes though. To create a custom scope, you must implement the following four methods.

a) Object get (String scopeName, ObjectFactory objFactory). The function returns an object from the core scope. Before creating the scope-object, any existence of the object should be checked and destroyed if found before creating a new custom scope.
b) Object destroy (String scopeName). This function destroys

the bean as soon as the defined scope expires for the bean. For a session scope bean, when the session ends, the bean is destroyed.

c) void registerDestructionCallback (String scopeName, Runnable dstrcnCallback). This function registers any callbacks when the destroy() method has completed its job.
d) String getConversionId(). This function returns the conversion identifier for each scope.

Before you can use the custom scopes, they have to be registered using the registerScope () function. The syntax is registerScope (String scopeName, Scope objScope). Once the scope is successfully registered, you can use it to define the bean scope.

153: What is the default bean scope in Spring and how will you modify it?

Answer:

The default bean scope is Singleton. It can be changed by setting "singleton" attribute to "false".

<bean id="bean1" class="..."

154: What are the types of Bean Scopes supported by Spring?

Answer:

The types of Bean Scopes supported by Spring are:

a) **Singleton**
    i) Default
    ii) Container creates only one instance of the bean and returns the shared instance to all the requests for the

singleton bean

iii) Shared instance is stored in the cache of all the singleton beans and returned to the subsequent requests for the singleton bean

iv) The shared bean instance is injected into each collaborating beans

v) Used for stateless bean

b) **Prototype**

i) A new bean instance is created for each and every request for the prototype bean

ii) Used for stateful bean

iii) To inject prototype bean into singleton bean, Lookup Method Injection can be used

c) **Request**

i) Request, session and globalsession scopes are available for web aware ApplicationContext implementation such as XmlWebApplicationContext

ii) If it is used for ClassPathXmlApplicationContext, it will throw IllegalStateException stating unknown bean scope

iii) Scope within Http Request. The request scope bean will be discarded when the request completes processing

d) **Session**

i) Scope within the lifetime of a single HttpSession

e) **global Session**

i) Used for portlet based web application

ii) Scope within the lifetime of a global portlet session

f) **Custom scope** can also be generated by using registerScope() method declared in the ConfigurableBeanFactory interface

155: What will happen if you inject prototype bean into singleton bean?

Answer:

a) Singleton bean is created only once so the prototype bean which is injected will also be created once at the instantiation of singleton bean

b) Hence same instance of prototype bean will be used for each request

c) If any changes required to the container managed bean instance meaning that, if the new instance of prototype bean needs to be created for each request at runtime, Method Injection can be used as below

d) <lookup-method name="..." bean="...">

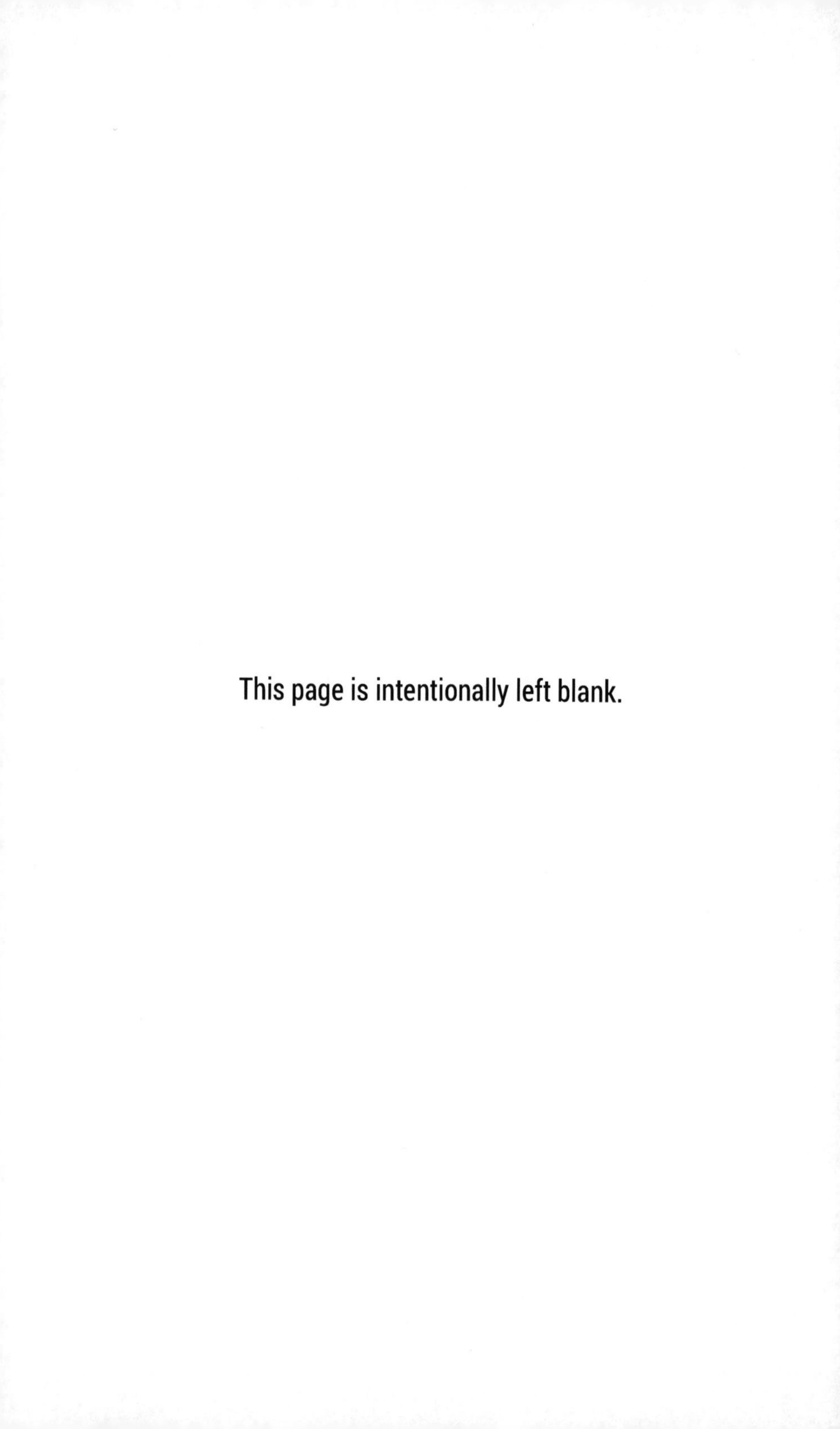

This page is intentionally left blank.

Chapter **22**

Bean Lifecycle Methods

Initialization Callbacks

156: How will you make the bean to do certain processes/actions upon initialization of the beans programmatically?

Answer:

a) We can make the bean to do certain processes/actions upon initialization of the beans programmatically by implementing "org.springframework.beans.factory.InitializingBean" interface in the bean class and override afterPropbrtiesSet() method

b) Disadvantage is that it is tightly coupled with spring

```
public class Animal implements InitializingBean {
    public void afterPropertiesSet() {
        ...
```

```
        }
    }
```

157: How will you create the bean to do certain actions upon initialization of the beans through XML configuration file?

Answer:

a) We can create the bean to do certain actions upon initialization of the beans through XML configuration file by including "init-method" attribute in <bean> tag
b) Doing some actions upon Initialization after all the properties of the bean have been set by the container

```
<bean id="..." class="com.ks.Test" init-
method="callInitMtd" />

public class Test {
    Public void callInitMtd() {
        ...
    }
}
```

Destruction Callbacks

158: How will you make the bean to do certain processes/actions upon destruction of the beans programmatically?

Answer:

a) We can make the bean to do certain processes/actions upon destruction of the beans programmatically by implementing "org.springframework.beans.factory.DisposableBean" interface in the bean class and override destroy() method

b) Disadvantage is that it is tightly coupled with spring

```
public class Animal implements InitializingBean {
    public void destroy() {
        ...
    }
}
```

159: How will you create the bean to do certain actions upon destruction of the beans through XML configuration file?

Answer:

a) We can create the bean to do certain actions upon destruction of the beans through XML configuration file by including "destroy-method" attribute in <bean> tag.

b) Doing some actions upon destruction meaning that when container containing the bean is destroyed.

```
<bean id="..." class="com.ks.Test" destroy-
method="callDestroyMtd" />
public class Test {
    Public void callDestroyMtd () {
        ...
    }
}
```

Annotation Callbacks

160: What are the annotations used for the beans to accomplish certain tasks upon initialization and destruction?

Answer:

The annotations used for the beans to accomplish certain tasks upon initialization and destruction are:

a) Using @PostConstruct for Initialization
b) Using @PreDestroy for destruction

161: What are the options available for controlling bean lifecycle behavior?

Answer:

The various options available for controlling bean lifecycle behavior are:

a) Using Custom init() and destroy () methods through init-method and destroy-method attributes
b) Implementing InitializingBean and DisposableBean interfaces and overriding afterPropertiesSet() and destroy() methods
c) Using @PostContruct and @PreDestroy annotations in the appropriate methods

162: What is the execution order for bean Initialization if multiple lifecycle mechanisms are configured for the same bean?

Answer:

The execution order for bean Initialization if multiple lifecycle mechanisms are configured for the same bean is:

a) Annotations – Method annotated with @PostConstruct
b) Implementing bean interface InitializingBean and overriding afterPropertiesSet() method

c) Custom init() method written in the bean class by using init-method attribute in <bean> tag

163: What is the execution order for bean Destruction if multiple lifecycle mechanisms are configured for the same bean?

Answer:

The execution order for bean Destruction if multiple lifecycle mechanisms are configured for the same bean is:

a) Annotations – Method annotated with @PreDestroy
b) Implementing bean interface DisposableBean and overriding destroy() method
c) Custom destroy() method written in the bean class by using destroy-method attribute in the <bean> tag

164: Is it possible for a bean object to define its own lifecycle methods/requirements.

Answer:

Yes, it is the execution order for bean Destruction if multiple lifecycle mechanisms are configured for the same bean using Lifecycle interface and LifecycleProcessor interface which extends Lifecycle interface. ApplicationContext delegates the control to the LifecycleProcessor which contains the methods for refreshing and closing of context.

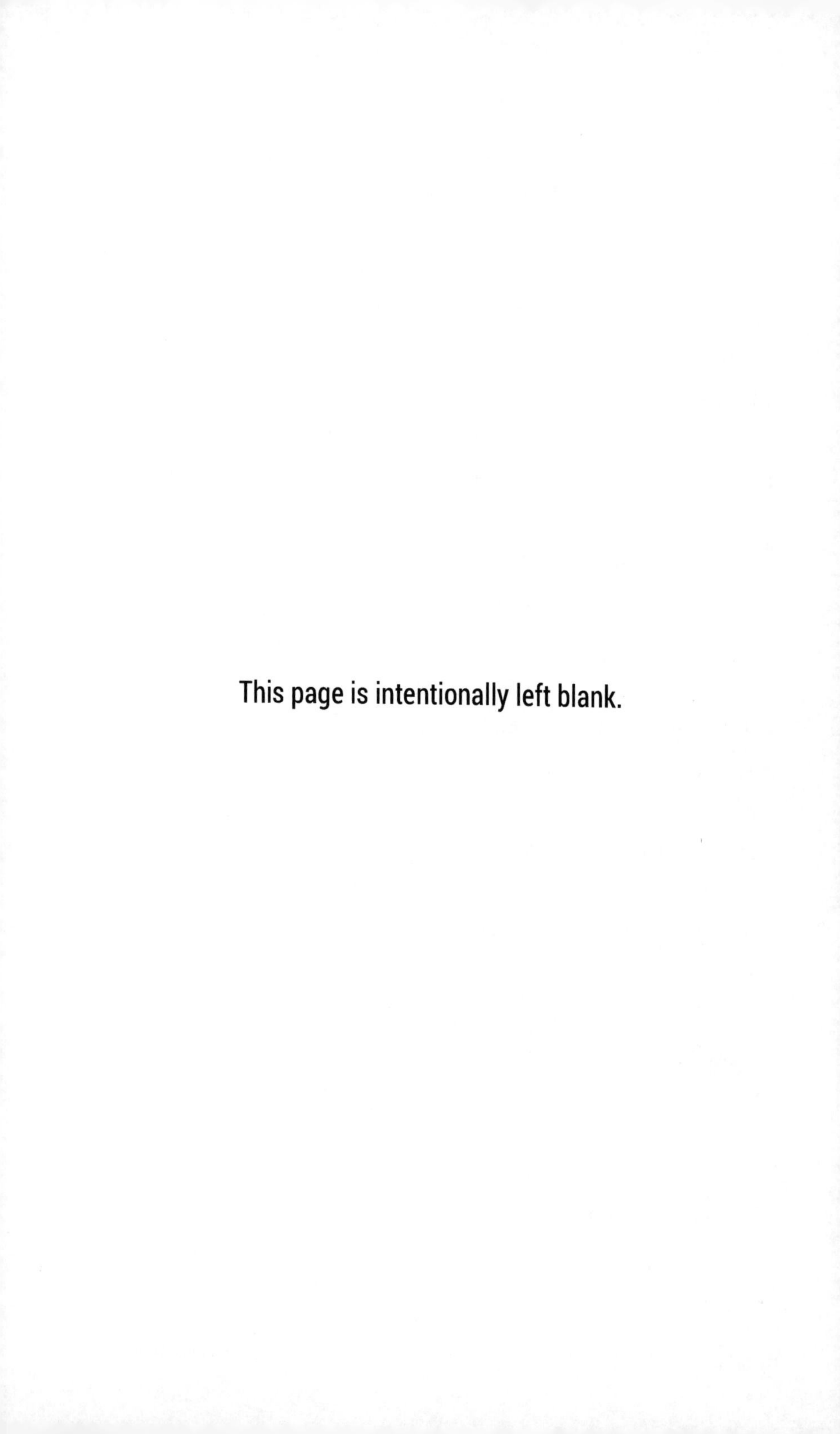
This page is intentionally left blank.

Chapter **23**

Inheritance (Normal Inheritance)

165: How do you create an inheritance template?

Answer:

An Inheritance Template can be considered like an Abstract base class. To create an Inheritance Template, you can use the bean tag without the *class* attribute and set the *abstract* attribute to *true*. In the derived class, the base class has to be mentioned in the *parent* attribute.

```
<bean id="myBaseBean" abstract="true">
    <property name="BeanName" value="Base Bean" />
</bean>
<bean id = "myDerivedBean" parent = "myBaseBean" class =
"<class_path>">
    <property name="BeanId" value="1010" />
```

```
    <property name="BeanName" value="Derived Bean" />
</bean>
```

166: Explain how to create an Abstract Bean and what is its use?

Answer:

To create an Abstract Bean, you can use the bean tag and set the value of *abstract* attribute to *true*. Do not mention the *class* attribute. This will make sure that the bean is not instantiated. Once the bean is made abstract, it can used as an inheritance template. Just as we use the Abstract classes in POJO, abstract beans can be used in Spring to create a base class with common properties for inheritance. The parent bean need not have class attributes and the common properties can be overridden in the derived beans.

```
<bean id="myPersonBean" abstract="true">
    <property name="PersonName" value="First Name, Last
    Name" />
</bean>
<bean id = "myCustomerBean" parent = "myPersonBean" class =
"<class_path>">
    <property name="myCustId" value="1010" />
    <property name="PersonName" value="Smith, Allen" />
    <property name="myCustCountry" value="USA" />
</bean>
```

Here, the base bean myPersonBean is declared with abstract = true.

167: What is a pure inheritance template?

Answer:

When the base abstract bean is used only to share some common attributes or values, it is known as pure inheritance template. In the following example,

```
<bean id="myPersonBean" abstract="true">
    <property name="PersonName" value="First Name, Last
    Name" />
</bean>
<bean id = "myCustomerBean" parent = "myPersonBean" class =
"<class_path>">
    <property name="myCustId" value="1010" />
    <property name="myCustCountry" value="USA" />
</bean>
```

The derived bean myCustomerBean will automatically inherit the PersonName attribute and value from the myPersonBean bean. If the myCustomerBean has overridden the PersonName attribute, then it will be considered for the derived class. When the base class contains all the shared attributes and the derived classes decide to skip them, the base class is called a pure inheritance template.

168: How will you implement inheritance in Spring?

Answer:

Inheritance can be implemented in Spring:

a) Using “parent” attribute in <bean> tag

```
<bean id=″bean1″ class=″...″ >
    <property name=″dbname″ value=″abc″ />
</bean>
<bean id=″bean2″ class=″...″ parent=″bean1″ >
    <property name=″uname″ value=″def″ />
```

</bean>

b) Instantiate the parent bean class as below

Test t = (Test) actxt.getBean ("bean1");

Chapter **24**

Inheritance with Abstract

169: How will you prevent the base class from being instantiated?

Answer:

We can prevent the base class from being instantiated using "abstract" attribute in parent <bean> tag.

170: Explain about Inheritance with Abstract attribute.

Answer:

If base class does not need to be instantiated, abstract attribute can be used. It will not allow the base class to be instantiated and will throw exception if it is instantiated. If abstract is not mentioned the container (ApplicationContext) will preinstantiate the bean.

```
<bean id="bean1" class="..." abstract="true" >
    <property name="dbname" value="abc" />
</bean>
```

```
<bean id="bean2" class="..." parent="bean1" >
    <property name="uname" value="def" />
</bean>
```

171: What will happen if you try to instantiate a bean that is declared as abstract in xml file?

Answer:

If we try to instantiate a bean that is declared as abstract in xml file, it will throw an exception "BeanIsAbstractException", is instantiated as below.

```
Test t = (Test) actxt.getBean ("bean1");
```

172: How will you override base class property in subclass through Xml configuration file?

Answer:

We can override base class property in subclass through XML configuration file as below:

```
<bean id="bean1"  abstract="true" ><!-- No need for class attribute
-- >
    <property name="dbname" value="abc" />
</bean>
<bean id="bean2" class="..." parent="bean1" >
    <property name="dbname" value="def" /> <! --Overriding
    property dbname -- >
</bean>
```

173: How will you define the bean's property value into a separate file instead of configuration XML file?

Answer:

We can define the bean's property value into a separate file instead of configuration XML file by:

a) **Using "PropertyPlaceholderConfigurer" class:**

```
<bean class =
"org.springframework.beans.factory.config.PropertyPlace
holderConfigurer">

    <property name="locations"
        value ="classpath:/java/prop/bean.properties" />

</bean>
```

b) **Using "context" namespace: (From Spring 2.5)**

```
<context:property-placeholder
location="classpath:/java/prop/bean.properties "/>
```

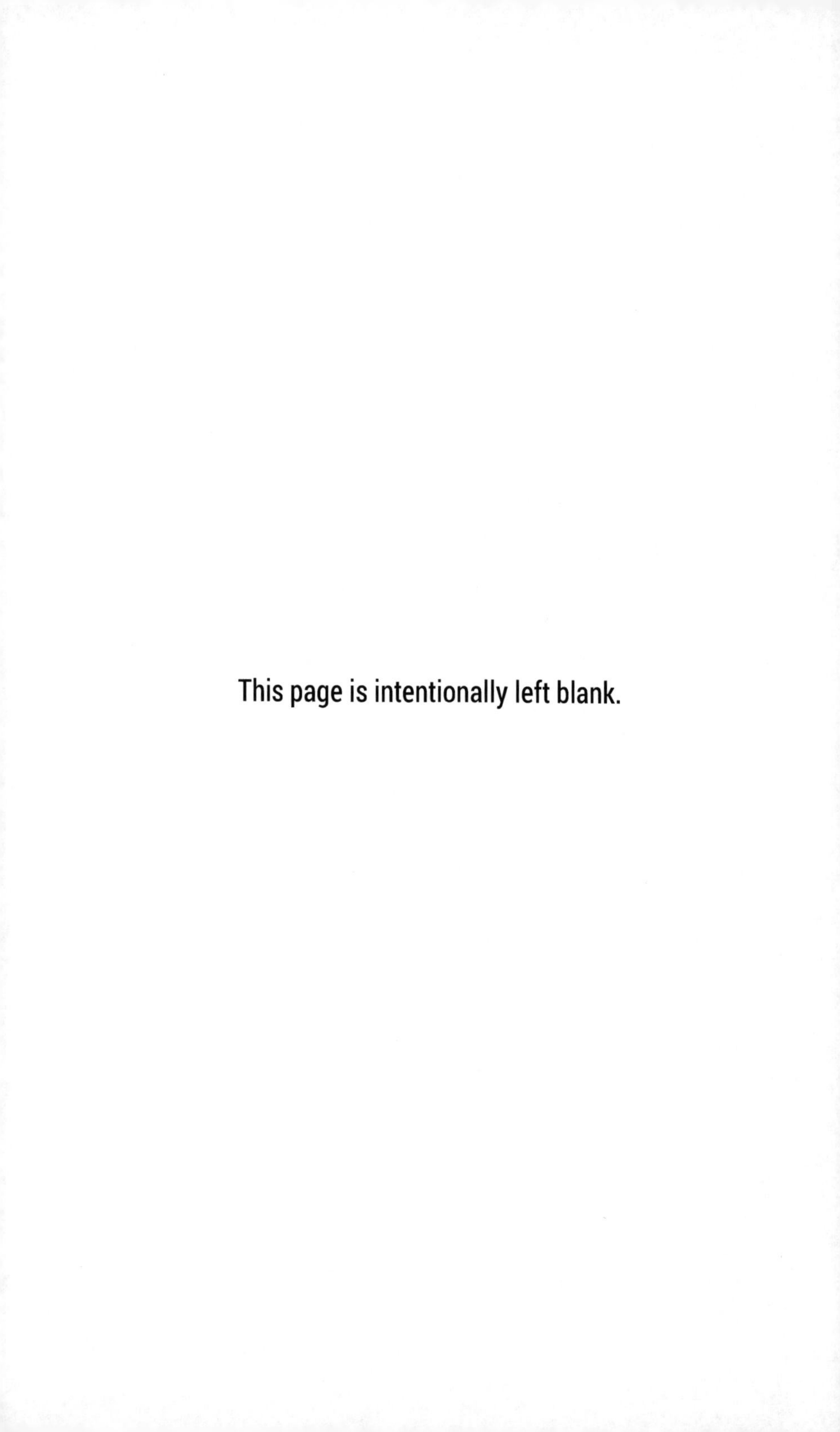

This page is intentionally left blank.

Chapter **25**

Annotations Based Configuration

174: Give an example of some annotations being supported by different versions of Spring.

Answer:

The annotations supported by different versions of Spring are:

a) **Spring 2.0:** @Required for enforcing required bean – applies to properties setter method

b) **Spring 2.5:**

   i) @Autowired - applies to setter method, non setter,method,properties, and constructor

   ii) JSR-250 annotations such as @PostConstruct, @PreDestroy, @Resource

   iii) @Component is a generic stereo type

   iv) @Service, @Repository and @Controller are

specializations of @Component and they are used in service layer, persistent layer and presentation layer respectively

c) **Spring 3.0:** JSR-330 such as @Inject, @Qualifier, @Named, @Provider which are in javax.inject package and JSR 330 jar should be present in classpath

175: How can the spring annotations be registered implicitly and autodetect component scanning?

Answer:

The spring annotations can be registered implicitly and autodetect component scanning by including below tag in configuration xml file:

a) <context:annotation-config/>
b) <context:component-scan base-package="test" />

176: Which properties can have @Autowired annotation?

Answer:

The following properties can have @Autowired annotation:

a) Setter method (required attribute can be set to true/false)
b) Collection properties (setter method of collection properties)
c) Concrete method (also with multiple arguments)
d) Constructors and fields (instance variables)

177: How will you prevent the failure of Autowiring when there are no beans to autowire?

Answer:

a) By default, autowire will fail if no beans are available for Autowiring
b) To prevent the failure by setting 'false' to "required" attribute of "@Autowired" annotation

```
@Autowired (required=false)
Public void setUsername(String username) {
    ...
}
```

178: Can we use @Autowired annotation for interfaces?

Answer:

Yes. @Autowired annotation is used for interfaces such as BeanFactory, ApplicationContext, ApplicationEventPublisher, ResourceLoader and MessageSource.

The other interfaces such as ConfigurableApplicationContext, ResoucePatternResolver that extend from above interfaces will also be resolved automatically without requiring any further set up.

```
{
    @Autowired
    Private ApplicationContext actxt;
    ...
}
```

179: What is the use of @Qualifier annotation?

Answer:

@Qualifier annotation is used to identify the specific bean to be autowired, when more than one bean has same type.

```
{
    @Autowired
    @Qualifier ("bean1")
    Private Emp emp;
    ...
}
<bean id="bean1" class="com.ks.Emp" />
<bean id="bean2" class="com.ks.Emp" />
```

Chapter **26**

ApplicationContext

180: How will you close the Spring IoC Container in the non-web applications?

Answer:

We can close the Spring IoC Container in the non-web applications by invoking registerShutdownHook() method of ApplicationContext.

ApplicationContext ac = new ClassPathXmlApplicationContext(
new String[] {"actxt.xml"});
ac.registerShutdownHook();

181: How will you create declarative ApplicationContext instance?

Answer:

a) We can create declarative ApplicationContext instance by configuring ContextLoaderListener and

ContextLoaderServlet in XML file

b) Context listener is executed after the servlet context is created for a web application hence it will be available for the first request and when the context is about to be shut down

```
<context-param>
    <param-name>contextConfigLocation</param-name>
    <param-value>
        /WEB-INF/applnCtxt1.xml, /WEB-INF/
        applnCtxt2.xml
    </param-value>
</context-param>

<listener>
    <listener-class>
        org.springframework.web.context.ContextLoaderL
        istener
    </listener-class>
</listener>
```

182: How will you access the properties file programmatically?

Answer:

Get the properties using FileSystemResource and set it in Location attribute of PropertyPlaceholderConfigurer class.

```
PropertyPlaceholderConfigurer pphc = new
PropertyPlaceholderConfigurer();
pphc.setLocation ( new FileSystemResource("appln.properties"));
```

183: How would you get ApplicationContext using ApplicationContextAware?

Answer:

We can get ApplicationContext using ApplicationContextAware with the following steps:

a) Write a class that implements ApplicationContextAware interface
b) Override setApplicationContext(ApplicationContext ac) method
c) Initialize this bean class in the configuration file

184: What methods will be overridden if BeanPostProcessor is used? Explain.

Answer:

The methods that will be overridden if BeanPostProcessor is used are:

a) postProcessBeforeInitialization() and postProcessAfterInitialization() methods
b) Write a class that implements BeanPostProcessor interface and override aforementioned methods
c) Initialize this bean class in the configuration file
d) These methods will be invoked at the pre and post initialization of all the beans

185: What URL prefixes can be used in getResource() method of ApplicationContext?

Answer:

The URL prefixes that can be used in getResource() method of

ApplicationContext are:

a) **classpath:** Files will be loaded from the classpath
b) **file:** Loaded from the filesystem as a URL
c) **ftp:** Access the resource through FTP protocol
d) **http**: Loaded as a URL, access the resource through HTTP

Example:

```
actxt.getResource("file:/ks/test.txt");
actxt.getResource("ftp:/ks/test.txt");
actxt.getResource("http:/ks/test.txt");
actxt.getResource("classpath:/ks/test.txt");
```

Chapter 27

Spring and Hibernate Integration

186: How will you configure JNDI in spring?

Answer:

We can configure JNDI in Spring using JndiObjectFactoryBean.

```
<bean id="dsrc"
    class=" org.springframework.jndi.JndiObjectFactoryBean">
    <property name="jndiName">
        <value>java:jdbc/TestSpring</value>
    </property>
</bean>
```

187: How will you integrate iBatis with Spring?

Answer:

We can integrate iBatis with Spring using SqlMapClientFactoryBean.

```
<bean id="sqlMapClientConf"
        class="org.springframework.orm.ibatis.SqlMapClientFacto
        ryBean">
    <property name="configLocation">
        <value>/WEB-INF/SqlMapConfig.xml</value>
    </property>

    <property name="dataSource">
        <ref bean="dsrc"/>
    </property>
</bean>
```

188: How will you configure hibernate mapping file in Spring configuration file?

Answer:

The steps to configure hibernate mapping file in Spring configuration file are:

a) Define LocalSessionFactoryBean in spring applicationContext.xml file
b) Define hibernate mapping file path in the "mappingResources" property (name) of LocalSessionFactoryBean

189: How will you configure/inject hibernate properties file in spring?

Answer:

The steps to configure/inject hibernate properties file in spring are:

a) Define PropertyPlaceholderConfigurer in spring application context file

b) Configure hibernate properties file path in the "locations" property of PropertyPlaceholderConfigurer

```
<bean id="pconfig"
class="org.springframework.beans.factory.config.PropertyPlaceho
lderConfigurer">
    <property name="locations">
        <list>
            <value>classpath:
            /hibprop/hibernate.properties</value>
        </list>
    </property>
</bean>
```

190: How will you define hibernate properties in Spring ApplicationContext file?

Answer:

We can define hibernate properties in Spring ApplicationContext file as follows:

```
<bean id="sessionFactory"
class="org.springframework.orm.hibernate3.LocalSessionFactory
Bean">
    <property name="hibernateProperties">
        <props>
            <prop key="hibernate.show_sql">. </prop>
            <prop key="hibernate.dialect"> . </prop>
        </props>
    </property>
</bean>
```

191: How will you integrate struts with spring?

Answer:

We can integrate struts with spring as follows:

a) Register ContextLoaderPlugIn in struts configuration file struts-config.xml
b) Give spring configuration file's path in "contextConfigLocation" property of the plug-in
c) Get spring beans using getWebApplicationContext() method

```
<struts-config>
    ...
    <plug-in
    className="org.springframework.web.struts.ContextLoaderP
    lugIn">
        <set-property property= "contextConfigLocation"
            value= "/WEB-INF/spring.xml" />
    </plug-in>
    ...
</struts-config>
```

Chapter 28

Spring AOP

192: What are the terminologies used in AOP?

Answer:

The terminologies used in AOP are:

a) Aspect
b) Join point
c) Advice
d) Pointcut
e) AOP Proxy

193: What is AOP?

Answer:

AOP stands for Aspect Oriented Programming. Aspects enable modularization of cross cutting concerns such as Transaction Management. It is used to intercept some processes and execute certain functionalities. E.g. Logging, Authentication.

194: What is meant by Aspects?

Answer:

Aspect is implemented using simple classes for which beans will be configured in spring XML file. It modularizes cross cutting concerns meaning that this classes can contain some common functionality which is required in many classes.

195: Explain about Advice.

Answer:

Advice is an action taken by an aspect at a particular join point (before and after method execution). The different types of advice are "before", "after", "around". Advice is considered as an interceptor.

196: What is Join point and Pointcut?

Answer:

Join point is point when advice(action) to be executed. Join point always represents execution of a method. Pointcut is a predicate that matches join point meaning that which method should be intercepted by regular expression pattern or method name.
For instance, execute a method (Join point) which contains certain name (Pointcut).

197: How will you define aop "advice" when the bean name of PlatformTransactionManager is given with some other name instead of "transactionManager"?

Answer:

It is defined using "transaction-manager" attribute in the tag

<tx:advice/> transactional advice.

```
    <tx:advice id="advice1" transaction-manager="txmgr">
    ...
    </tx:advice>
```

198: How will you define pointcut and advisor if you want to execute the advice before executing any of the methods from a class/an interface?

Answer:

Pointcut and advisor is defined as follows:

```
<aop:config>
    <aop:pointcut id="pcut"
        expression="execution(* com.java.EmplService.*(..))"/>
    <aop:advisor advice-ref="advice1" pointcut-ref="pcut"/>
</aop:config>
```

199: How will you make your advice to execute certain methods, for instance, starting with "get" in read-only transaction?

Answer:

All methods starting with "get" such as getUser() will be executed with the read-only transaction and the other methods with the default transaction.

```
<tx:advice id="advice1" transaction-manager="txmgr">
    <tx:attributes>
        <tx:method name="get*" read-only="true"/>
        <tx:method name="*"/>
    </tx:attributes>
</tx:advice>
```

200: How will you rollback the declarative transaction using aop?

Answer:

We can roll back the declarative transaction using aop using "rollback-for" and "no-rollback-for" attributes in <tx:advice> transaction advice.

```
<tx:advice id="advice1" >
    <tx:attributes>
        <tx:method name="get*"
            rollback-for="Throwable"
            no-rollback-for="ProductNotFoundException"
        />
    </tx:attributes>
</tx:advice>
```

201: How will you enable annotation transaction management in spring AOP?

Answer:

We can enable annotation transaction management in spring aop using <tx:annotation-driven/> tag in spring configuration file and using @Transactional annotation in the POJO class.

XML file:

```
<tx:annotation-driven transaction-manager="txmgr"/>
```

POJO class:

```
@Transactional
public class UserService {
...
}
```

202: Give some examples of Spring AOP.

Answer:

Some examples of Spring AOP are:

a) Transaction Management
b) Security Management
c) Logging (Program loggers)
d) Profiling (Calculating the program execution time)
e) Tracing (Tracing what are the methods being called in a program)

203: What are the types of Advice?

Answer:

The different types of Advice are:

a) **Before Advice:** Executes an advice before executing a join point
b) **After Returning Advice:** Executes an advice after executing a join point if it completes normally without an exception
c) **After Throwing Advice:** Executes an advice, if any exception occurs in join point
d) **Around advice:** Executes an advice before and after executing a join point. It will be able to choose whether to proceed to join point or stop the method execution

204: How will you implement Around Advice?

Answer:

The steps to implement Around Advice are:

a) Write a interceptor class implementing MethodInterceptor

Interface

b) Override invoke() method which is of return type "Object" and argument type as "MethodInvocation"

c) To continue with the normal execution flow meaning that to continue from interceptor to joinpoint, invoke proceed() method on the MethodInvocation object

Object obj = minv.proceed();

205: How do you implement AOP Proxy?

Answer:

The steps to implement AOP Proxy are:

a) Define ProxyFactoryBean in the spring configuration file by using its class "org.springframework.aop.framework.ProxyFactoryBean"

b) Inject the bean reference of the class which implements pointcut, into the "target" property

c) Inject the interceptor bean reference into "interceptorNames" property

206: What is Advisor in AOP?

Answer:

Advisor in AOP combines Pointcut and Advice into a single unit using "DefaultPointcutAdvisor" and pass it to ProxyFactoryBean using the properties "target" and "interceptorNames".

207: How will you implement Advisor?

Answer:

The steps to implement Advisor are:

a) Define pointcut using "NameMatchMethodPointcut" class and give the method name (which needs to be intercepted) in "mappedName" property
b) Define advice using bean class which contains pointcut methods
c) Inject these pointcut and advice bean reference into the properties "pointcut" and "advice" of "DefaultPointcutAdvisor" class
d) Inject the advisor bean reference into the "interceptorNames" property of "ProxyFactoryBean"

208: How will you define pointcut and advice into single bean?

Answer:

We can define pointcut and advice into single bean using NameMatchMethodPointcutAdvisor class and give pointcut method name in "mappedName" property and advice bean class reference in "advice" property.

```
<bean id="bean1"
    class="org.springframework.aop.support.NameMatchMethod
    PointcutAdvisor">
    <property name="mappedName" value="getUname" />
    <property name="advice" ref="advice1" />
</bean>
```

209: What will you do if you want to apply advice to the pointcut method which contains the word "dao" with the method name?

Answer:

Using "RegexpMethodPointcutAdvisor" class, we can intercept all the pointcut method which has the word "dao" with the name or intercept all the DAO classes.

```
<bean id="advisor1"
    class="org.springframework.aop.support.RegexpMethodPoint
    cutAdvisor">
    <property name="patterns">
        <list>
            <value>.*DAO.*</value>
        </list>
    </property>
    <property name="advice" ref="advice1" />
</bean>
```

210: How will you avoid creating many proxy factory beans in spring AOP?

Answer:

We can avoid creating many proxy factory beans in spring AOP using "BeanNameAutoProxyCreator", give bean names in "beanNames" property and advisor bean id in "interceptorNames" property.

```
<beanclass="org.springframework.aop.framework.autoproxy.Bean
NameAutoProxyCreator">
    <property name="beanNames">
        <list>
            <value>*Dao</value>
        </list>
    </property>
    <property name="interceptorNames">
```

```
        <list>
            <value>advisor1</value>
        </list>
    </property>
</bean>
```

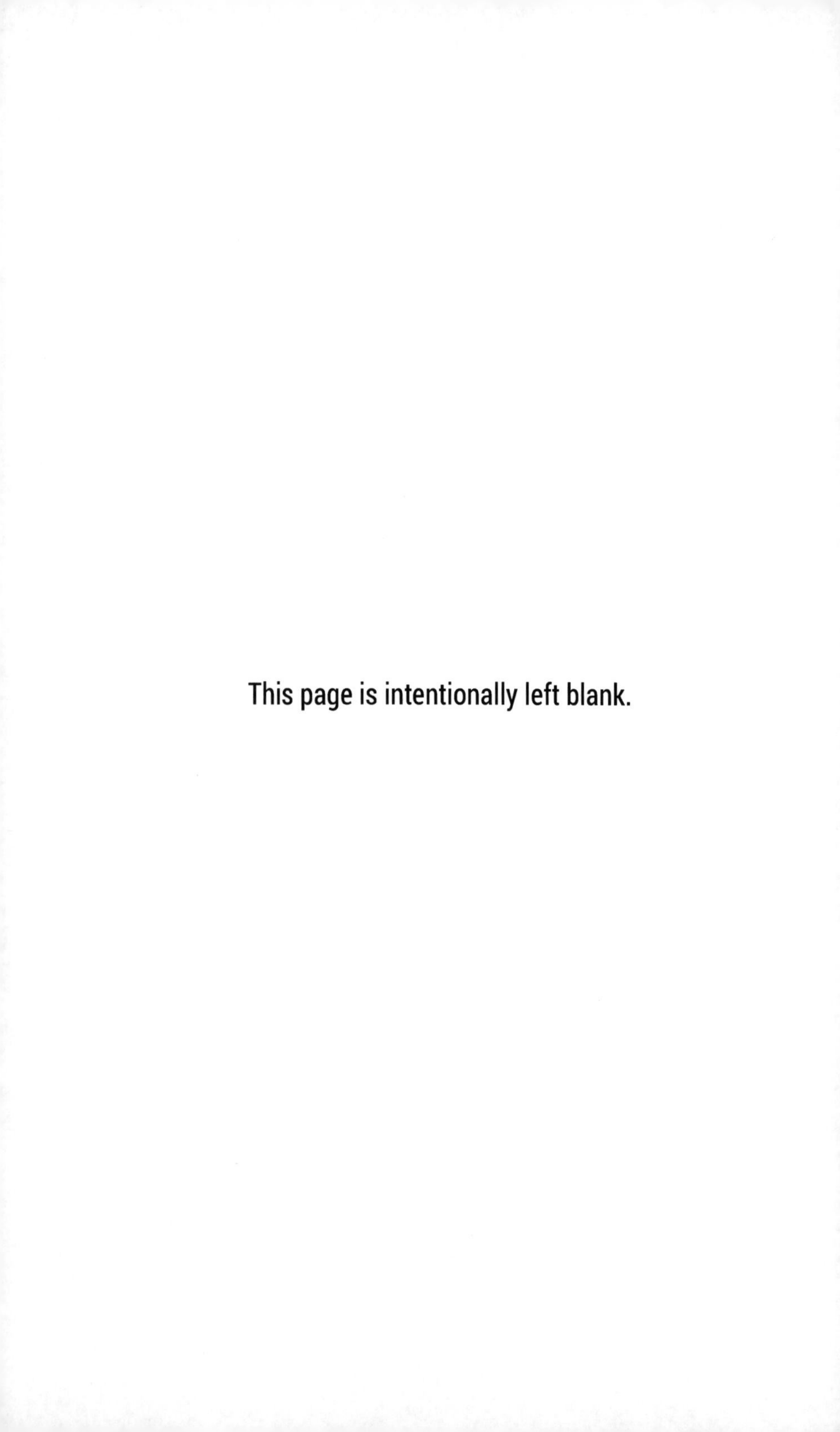
This page is intentionally left blank.

Struts

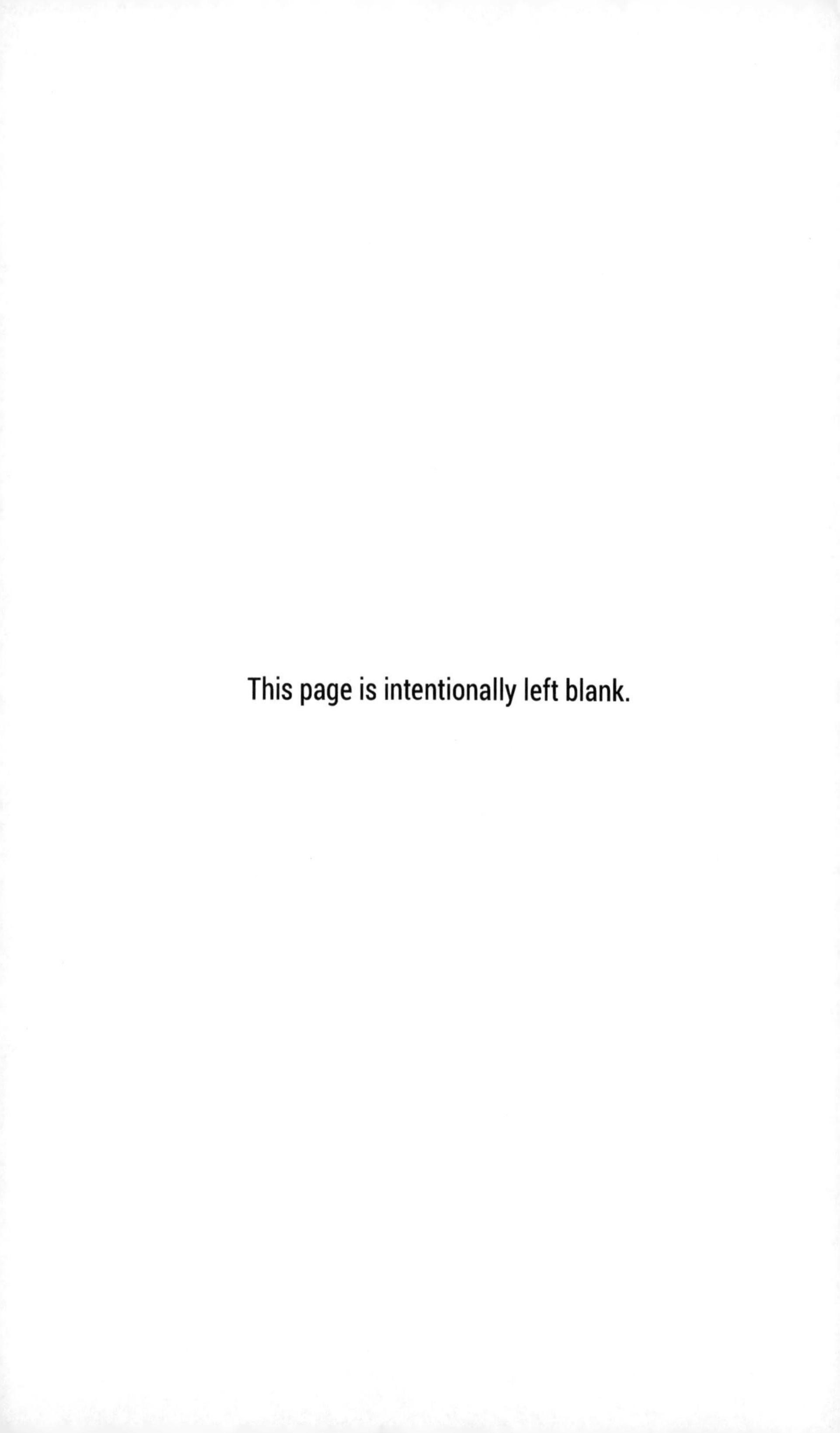
This page is intentionally left blank.

Chapter **29**

Configuration

211: What is the purpose of the following files in Struts?

a) web.xml
b) struts-default.xml
c) struts-plugin.xml

Answer:

These are the Struts configuration files.

a) **web.xml** – This configuration file contains all the framework details of the web application. All Application level parameters, such as the FileDispatcher, the filter class etc. are configured here. This is a mandatory file.
b) **struts-default.xml** – This configuration file contains the default configuration details provided by Struts. This file is included into the struts.xml file so that all default parameters are loaded automatically. You can change the configuration and include your own default xml file

instead. It is an optional file.

c) **struts-plugin.xml** – This configuration file contains the optional configuration details about the Plugins and is similar to the struts.xml.

212: How do you manage multiple configuration files in struts?

Answer:

You can create as many configuration files in Struts. All you have to do is to include them in your struts.xml file so that they can be referenced when required. The following is the code snippet for changing the struts.xml file

```
<struts>

<package name="myDefaultPackage" namespace="/"
extends="struts-default">
</package>

<include file="xyz/struts-xyz.xml"></include>
<include file="abc/struts-abc.xml"></include>

</struts>
```

Now the individual custom xml files have to be created.

For struts-xyz.xml

```
<struts>

<package name="xyz" namespace="/xyz" extends="struts-default">
    <action name="Welcome to xyz!" class="<class_path>">
        <result>welcomeXyz.jsp</result>
```

```
    </action>
</package>
</struts>
```

For struts-abc.xml

```
<struts>

<package name="abc" namespace="/abc" extends="struts-default">
    <action name="Welcome to abc!" class="<class_path>">
        <result>welcomeAbc.jsp</result>
    </action>
</package>
</struts>
```

213: What is the flow of requests in struts application?

Answer:

The flow of requests in struts application are as follows:

a) The request goes to the web.xml file where ActionServlet is configured. Struts-config.xml file's path is given in the <init-param> of ActionServlet.
b) ActionServlet will search the struts-config.xml file to verify whether any matching action class is found for the specified URL path
c) If the action class is available, it will find out the appropriate form bean using the "name" attribute of the <action> tag. The form beans will be present inside <form-beans> tag

d) It creates an instance for the actionform and call its getters and setters method to process the request parameters
e) Then it will call the validate() method of the form bean to validate all the parameters before forwarding to the action class
f) To achieve this, the "validate" attribute should be set to "true" and "input" attribute should be given as the input JSP name
g) The form bean populates the ActionErrors object in case of errors and return back to the ActionServlet. That is, if any field value entered does not pass the validation criteria, it will populate the ActionErrors with the error message
h) ActionServlet then check the ActionErrors returned by the form beans. If any error occurred, the originating JSP page will be displayed with appropriate error message
i) If no error is found, control will go to Action class to execute its business logic and return the ActionForward object which in turn forwards the control to the next JSP/action class

Request → web.xml (ActionServlet) → struts-config.xml → action-mapping → actionform (form-beans) → validate() → action class → JSPpage

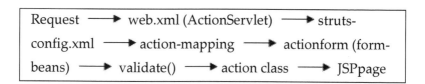

214: How many configuration files can be defined in a Struts application?

Answer:

More than one configuration files (struts-config.xml) can be defined in a Struts application.

a) Using comma delimited file names

```
<servlet>
    <servlet-name>actionServlet</servlet-name>
    <servlet-class>
        org.apache.struts.action.ActionServlet
</servlet-class>
    <init-param>
        <param-name>config</param-name>
        <param-value>
            /WEB-INF/struts-config.xml, /WEB-INF/struts-
            user.xml
        </param-value>
    </init-param>
        ...
</servlet>
<servlet-mapping>
    <servlet-name> actionServlet </servlet-name>
    <url-pattern>*.do</url-pattern>
</servlet-mapping>
```

215: What are the tags of "struts-config.xml" file?

Answer:

The tags of "struts-config.xml" file are:

a) **<form-beans> and <form-bean>**
b) **<global-exceptions> and <exception>**
c) **<global-forwards> and <forward>**
d) **<action-mappings> and <action>**
e) **<controller> :** For RequestProcessor

f) **<message-resources> :** Message resources
g) **<plug-in> :** To include plugin such as spring's ContextLoaderPlugIn

216: How can you make Message Resources Definitions file available to the Struts application?

Answer:

We can make Message Resources Definitions file available to the Struts application by:

a) Using <message-resources> tag in struts-config.xml file
b) <message-resources key="..." parameter="com.ks.MyAppMsgProperties" null="false"/>

217: How will you configure message resource file in the configuration file using ActionServlet?

Answer:

We can configure message resource file in the configuration file using ActionServlet by:

a) Using Actionservlet in web.xml
b) <servlet>

```
<servlet-name>action<servlet-name>
<servlet-
class>org.apache.struts.action.ActionServlet<servlet-
class>
<init-param>
    <param-name>application<param-name>
    <param-value>ks.resrc.myApplnResrc<param-
    value>
</init-param>
```

</servlet>

c) However this application resource file will be accessed by all the action classes and action forms since it is loaded with ActionServlet.

218: What XML parser is provided in struts to parse struts-config.xml file?

Answer:

'Digester' framework XML parser is provided in struts to parse struts-config.xml file.

219: How will you access message resource within Action class?

Answer:

We can access message resource within Action class by:

a) **Using MessageResources class and getResources() and getMessage() methods**

b) **Reading from ActionServlet**:

```
MessageResources applResrc =
this.getServlet().getResources();
```

c) **Reading from struts-config file**: (configured using <message-resources >)

```
MessageResources applResrc = getResources(req);
```

d) Messages are retrieved by using **applResrc.getMessage**("user.label")

220: What are the changes required to migrate struts1.x application to struts2.0?

Answer:

The changes required to migrate struts1.x application to struts2.0 are:

a) Change the servlet name in web.xml from ActionServlet (struts1.x) to FilterDispatcher (struts2)
b) Modify struts1.x configuration file "struts-config.xml" to Struts2 configuration file "struts.xml"
c) Modify struts 1.x ActionForm to Struts2 POJO class. The separate form bean class for each form is not required in struts2. The POJO class contains setter/getter methods and execute() method
d) Change struts 1.x action class which extends Action class to Struts2 Action classes which implements Action interface and extends ActionSupport class
e) The return type of execute() method is String in struts2 where as it is of type ActionForward in struts1.x
f) Instead of <forward> tag within <action> tag in struts1.x, <result type="redirect"> tag is being used in struts2
g) No need to use JSTL as in struts1.x. Struts2 contains separate tags

Chapter **30**

Main Classes (Action classes and ActionForms)

221: Explain the Action interface.

Answer:

In Struts 2, the Action interface is where all the business logic, data handling and responses are decided and programmed. The interface contains the following static variables with constant values and an execute method which has to be overridden to apply the business logic.

public static final String ERROR = "error", which notifies an error when the form was submitted.

public static final String LOGIN = "login", which notifies a login when the form was submitted.

public static final String NONE = "none", which notifies that there

was no action when the form was submitted.
public static final String SUCCESS = "success", which notifies a successful submission of the form.
public static final String INPUT = "input", which notifies an input when the form was submitted.

These constants can be used while applying the business logic.
public String execute() throws Exception
All the business logic has to be applied in the implementation of the execute() function which is mentioned in the struts.xml file to be called when a particular action form is submitted.
<action name = "<form_name>" class = "<class_path>" method = "execute">

The Class mentioned is the class that implements the execute() function and the form_name is the name of the form submitted by the user. For each web form, a different class and its execute() can be submitted.

222: What is StrictMethodInvocation or SMI?

Answer:

Strict Method Invocation makes sure that no other method, other than execute() and the ones specified under *<allowed-methods>* are called by a web form upon request or post. This restricts the wildcard method invocations also. The allowed methods can be specified explicitly comma separated within the *<allowed-methods>* *</allowed-methods>* tags in the struts.xml. For each package the *strict-method-invocation* attribute can be set to *false* to allow method invocation dynamically. By default it is *true* and it can be changed in the struts.xml configuration file. SMI allows specifying the allowed-methods for each action. If allowed-methods are not explicitly set, only the *global-allowed-methods* are dynamically invoked. If *strict-method-invocation* attribute is made *true*, all methods those fall under the *RegEx - ([A-Za-z0-9_$]*)* range will be available for dynamic invocation. You can change this range by changing the <*constant name="struts.strictMethodInvocation.methodRegex" value=*"<allowed_character_range>"/>. You can set the allowed_character_range to match your choice of methods to be allowed.

223: What are the advantages of extending the ActionSupport class?

Answer:

Even though we can implement the Action interface and the execute code in it for implementing business intelligence, extending the ActionSupport class is considered a better choice. The ActionSupport class implements the Action interface. So you can access the members of the Action interface even if you extend the ActionSupport class. Further, the validate() function in the ActionSupport class lets you include all business validations in it. It also has the getText() method that helps you get the localized text from the resource bundle. Further it also lets the user to handle any exception that is raised in the form request or submit.

224: What are the main classes used in struts application?

Answer:

The main classes used in struts application are:

a) **Action Class:** To process all the requests and return an object of type ActionForward
b) **ActionForm Class:** Mediator between model and view. Contains form properties
c) **ActionMapping Class**: Using <action> tag for each action class mappings
d) **ActionForward Class:** Identifies where the control will be forwarded
e) **ActionServlet Class:** Acts as a Front Controller

225: What is the role of ActionServlet in struts?

Answer:

The role of ActionServlet in struts is as follows:

a) Acts as Controller. Represents the 'C' in MVC architecture
b) Defined in web.xml file as below in <servlet> tag

```
<servlet-class>
    org.apache.struts.action.ActionServlet
</servlet-class>
```

c) To process the user requests
d) To retrieve data from the Model (M in MVC) to send it to View page (V in MVC)
e) To select the view page that needs to be sent to user
f) To initialize and clean up the resources

226: What are the types of Action classes?

Answer:

The different types of Action Classes are:

a) **DispatchAction:** To group the different methods into

single action class

b) **LookupDispatchAction:** Method name can differ from jsp form's button label
c) **ForwardAction:** To forward the control to another jsp/action classes
d) **IncludeAction:** To add the output of existing Servlet class in the current page
e) **SwitchAction:** To switch from one module to another module when multiple modules and multiple struts-config files are used
f) **DownloadAction:** To download a file by extending this action class and using getStreamInfo() method

227: What are the struts tag libraries?

Answer:

From struts 1.3 onwards, the configuration of the .tld files in web.xml using <taglib> tag is not required. It can be accessed by specifying its URI in jsp file as <%@taglib URI="..." prefix=".."/>.

a) **struts-html.tld:** To be included to use html form tags
b) **struts-bean.tld:** To access bean properties in the jsp using <bean:write> etc
c) **struts-logic.tld:** To use logic tags such as <logic:iterate>
d) **struts-nested.tld:** To use nested tags

228: Explain about IncludeAction class.

Answer:

IncludeAction class is:

a) Used to include the legacy programs into the existing

programs. That is, it is used to include the output of the existing servlet into the current jsp page (response of the struts application)

```
<action path="/existingServlet1"
    parameter="/ks/servlets/ExistingServlet1"
    type="org.apache.struts.actions.IncludeAction" />
```

b) Using parameter attribute, the actual servlet will be included in the response

229: Which class is used to forward the request in struts?

Answer:

a) ActionMapping class.
b) Represented in struts-config.xml file as <action-mappings> tag
c) Commons Digester component is used to parse this xml based properties/descriptions of the action mappings and creates and instantiates the appropriate objects for each action instances
d) Used for the controller servlet to know about how the request URI will be mapped to an appropriate action classes. That is, it indicates that the mappings between the request and the action class

230: How and where is the ActionMapping specified?

Answer:

ActionMapping is specified in struts-config.xml file.

```
<action-mappings>
    <action path="/addUser"
```

```
        type="user.userAction"
        name="addUserForm"
        input="/addUser.jsp"
        scope="request"
        validate="true">
        <forward name="succ" path="/confirmUser.jsp"/>
        <forward name="fail" path="/userError.jsp"/>
    </action>
</action-mappings>
```

231 What are the scopes of Form beans?

Answer:

a) Request and Session scopes.
b) Session is the default scope
c) If it is in Session scope, reset() method should be implemented in the form bean to initialize it for each time/use

232: What are the design patterns used by struts components?

Answer:

The design patterns used by struts components are:

a) **ActionServlet acts as Controller:** Command design pattern
b) **RequestProcessor's process() method:** Template Method design pattern
c) **Action class:** Adapter design pattern
d) **Struts Tiles:** Composite View
e) **J2ee patterns:**

i) MVC
ii) Service to Worker, Front Controller
iii) Dispatcher View
iv) View Helper
v) Synchronizer Token

233: How will you retrieve the values from JSP page if DynaActionForm is used?

Answer:

We can retrieve by struts components using the getter method of the properties in action class.

```
DynaActionForm userForm = (DynaActionForm) form;
String uname = (String) userForm.get("name");
Integer age = (String) userForm.get("age");
```

234 How will you add multiple Application messages properties file in struts-config.xml?

Answer:

```
<struts-config>
    ...
    <form-beans> ... </form-beans>
    ...
    <action-mappings> ... </action-mappings>
    <message-resources parameter="ApplMessages1.properties"/>
    <message-resources parameter=" ApplMessages2.properties
    "/>
</struts-config>
```

235: What will happen if name attribute of the <forward> in <action> tag is same as <global-forward> tag's <forward> name?

Answer:

a) <action> tag's <forward> takes high precedence

b) If <forward> is not given in <action> element, then <global-forward> will take place

236: Write down a code for validate() and reset() methods.

Answer:

```
public ActionErrors validate(ActionMapping actionMapping,
HttpServletRequest req) { ActionErrors errors = new
ActionErrors();
    if ((uname.equals(" ") && (uname == null) && (pwd == null)) {
        errors.add("loginError", new
        ActionMessage("loginError.required"));
    }
            return errors;
}
public void reset ( ActionMapping actionMapping,
HttpServletRequest req) {
    this.pwd = null;
    this.uname = null;
}
```

237: Which method is used to execute the business logic in struts application?

Answer:

a) The execute() method of return type ActionForward and having parameters such as ActionMapping, ActionForm,

HttpServletRequest and HttpServletResponse.

b) Used to process the requests and communicate with Model (database)
c) Used to update the variables and do validations and return the ActionForward object to forward the request appropriately

```
public ActionForward execute( ActionMapping actionMapping,
ActionForm form,
        HttpServletRequest req,
        HttpServletResponse resp) throws Exception{
    ...
}
```

238: What are the steps to write more than one related methods into single action class. For instance, to group the related methods such as add, update, delete into single action class?

Answer:

a) **Extend DispatchAction class**
b) **In Action class**: Write all the required methods having ActionForward as return type and parameters as execute() method
c) **In jsp**: Include the method name in the Query String along with action path as below

    action="userSearch.do?method=userIdSearch"
    action="userSearch.do?method=userNameSearch"

d) **In struts-config.xml:** Give parameter name which is used to store the method names.

```
<action path="/ userSearch"
    name="userForm"
    type="com.ks.action.UserAction"
    scope="request"
    validate="false"
    parameter="method">
    <forward name=".." path=".." />
</action>
```

239: Can we have parameterized constructor in ActionForm bean class?

Answer:

a) No. Default no argument constructor should be present
b) Must have public getter and setter methods for all the properties

240: How many instances will be created for an Action class in struts? Is action class thread-safe?

Answer:

a) Only one instance for each action class
b) It is not thread-safe
c) The container will create separate thread to process each request. Hence the instance/**class variable** of the action class is **not thread-safe**

241: What is DynaActionForm and explain the steps to use it?

Answer:

a) Allows the form properties to be created dynamically in

xml file rather than creating the separate ActionForm bean class for each JSP forms

b) Define the properties in struts-config.xml file as below
<form-bean name="MyUserForm"
type="org.apache.struts.action.DynaActionForm">
<form-property name="usrname"
type="java.lang.String"/>
<form-property name="usrage" type="java.lang.Integer"/>
</form-bean>

c) The container will not expect an ActionForm class for this form when it executes its action class in <action> tag

d) Retrieve the properties in Action class using its getter method
DynaActionForm MyUserForm = (DynaActionForm) form;
String usrname = (String) MyUserForm.get("usrname");
Integer usrage = (String) MyUserForm.get("usrage");

242: Can I have html form property without associating it with setters/getters methods of formbean?

Answer:

a) Yes. Using DynaActionForm defined in struts-config.xml file

b) Define DynaActionForm using <form-bean> tag within <form-beans> for the form which does not have separate form bean

c) If the form is not defined as DynaActionForm and it does not have ActionForm bean created, it will show error

243: Compare Struts1.0 and struts 1.1.

Answer:

a) Execute() method of struts1.1 replaces perform() method of struts1.0
b) DynaActionForm is introduced to avoid creating ActionForm bean class for each forms
c) Tiles framework is introduced to provide layout in JSP pages which minimizes coding
d) Our own controller can be written by extending RequestProcessor

244: How many ActionServlets are created in struts application?

Answer:

Only one ActionServlet for each web application. That is, only one instance for the ActionServlet will be created to process all the requests.

245: Why ActionServlet is singleton in Struts? Explain.

Answer:

ActionServlet is singleton in Struts as it:

a) Acts as a controller to process all the requests
b) Created based on the Singleton design pattern so that only one instance will be created for this servlet class. Multiple threads will be created to process each user request

246: How does the container know whether it is a struts or spring application?

Answer:

a) The container knows whether it is a struts or spring application using servlet name defined in the web.xml file
b) ActionServlet is defined for STRUTS application whereas DispatcherServlet is configured for SPRING application
c) Based on this servlet class, the container finds the configuration files accordingly

247: Explain about validate() and reset () methods.

Answer:

a) **Validate()**
    i) Used to validate all the form properties
    ii) Defined in ActionForm bean class
    iii) Executed before the control goes to Action class, if validation successful. Otherwise the control goes to ActionServlet which will redisplay the originating JSP
    iv) Returns ActionErrors as a collection of ActionError object
    v) public ActionErrors validate (ActionMapping actionMapping, HttpServletRequest req) { ... }
b) **reset()**
    i) Used to clear the form field values for each request before the new request
    ii) Defined in ActionForm bean class
    iii) public void reset(ActionMapping actionMapping, HttpServletRequest req) { }

248: Explain <global-forwards>.

Answer:

a) <global-forwards> is used to forward to another resources such as jsp/servlet action
b) If <forward> is not provided in the specific <action>, the JSP page which is given in the <global-forwards> will be displayed
c) The <forward> of <action> has high precedence over <global-forwards>
d) It is an instance of the ActionForward class returned from the execute() method of the action class
e) The attributes are name, path, redirect

249: What is the use of ForwardAction class?

Answer:

a) ForwardAction class is used to forward the request to another JSP/specified URL
b) No need to create separate action class
c) For instance, used if you want to forward from general index.jsp to application specific jsp page

```
<action path="/addUser"
    type="org.apache.struts.actions.ForwardAction"
    parameter="/jsp/userConfirm.jsp"
    input="/jsp/addUser.jsp"
    scope="request"
    validate="false">
</action>
```

250: What is the difference between ForwardAction and IncludeAction?

Answer:

a) **ForwardAction**
   i) Used to forward the request to specific URL
   ii) Type="org.apache.struts.actions.ForwardAction"
   iii) <html:link action=".." > is used in jsp to forward

b) **IncludeAction**
   i) Used to include an action into another action
   ii) Type="org.apache.struts.actions.IncludeAction"
   iii) <jsp:include page="/addUser.do" />is used in jsp to include
   iv) Forward cannot be used here since an action needs to be included into another action

Chapter **31**

Exception Handling

251: How is exception handling simplified in Struts?

Answer:

Struts uses the action result to redirect the application control to a different error page upon any error or exception. This way, you can show a different Error Page to the user when any error or exception is raised instead of showing it on the current page. The following code snippet in the struts.xml file helps explain exception handling.

```
<action name = "<actionclassname>" Class = "<class_path>"
method="execute">
    <exception-mapping exception = "<Exception_name>" result =
    "error" />
    <result name="success">/WelcomePage.jsp</result>
    <result name="error">/ErrorPage.jsp</result>
</action>
```

The actionclassname is the class which either extends the ActionSupport class or implements the Action interface. The execute method's implementation has to be there in this class. When the execute () method is executed, if any exception is raised the same is caught by the execution-mapping attribute. If the exception corresponds to the <Exception_Name>, the value of *result* is set to *"error"*. Based on the result, the WelcomePage or the ErrorPage is sent to the user.

252: Explain Specific and Generic Exception handling in Struts 2?

Answer:

a) **Handling specific exceptions**

   In this approach, in the struts-config.xml file, the following exception handling tag for a particular exception is added.

   ```
   <global-exceptions>
       <exception key = "exception_handler" type =
       "<Specific_Exception_Name>" path="<Error_Page>"/>
   </global-exceptions>
   ```

   Here the *exception_handler* will hold the actual exception thrown by the application and check it against the *Specific_Exception_Name*. If they match, the control goes to the *Error_Page* given in the *path* which displays the error message corresponding to the specific exception.

b) **Handling Generic exceptions**

   In this approach, apart from the specific exception handling, an additional checking for Generic exceptions is also given and if found, taken to a general error page.

```
<global-exceptions>
    <exception key = "exception_handler" type =
    "<Specific_Exception_Name>" path="<Error_Page>"/>
    <exception key = "exception_handler" type =
    "java.lang.Exception" path="<Common_Error_Page>"/>
</global-exceptions>
```

In this case, if the exception caught is not the one corresponding to the specific exception, the general handler will go to the generic exception *java.lang.Exception* and display the Common_Error_Page.

There is a third method for exception handling in Struts 2 which involves creating a subclass of *ExceptionHandler* and using a *custom_exception* in *global-exceptions*.

253: How are exceptions handled in Struts?

Answer:

Exceptions are handled in Struts by:

a) **Using Programmatic Exception handling:** Uses try-catch block in the code
b) **Using Declarative Exception handling:** Uses <global-exceptions> or <exception> tag within <action> tag
c) **Custom Exception handler:** Using "handler" attribute in <exception> tag

254: Can we handle exceptions in Struts programmatically?

Answer:

Yes. Write try- catch block explicitly in the code to handle exception. It is useful when some variable's value is needed in case of exceptions.

```
try {
    ...
}
Catch (IOException ioe) {
    ...
}
Catch (Exception ex) {
    ...
}
```

255: Explain Declarative exception handling.

Answer:

a) **Global Exception handling:**
   i) Define <global-exceptions> tag in the struts-config.xml file
   ii) Available to the whole application (all action classes)

b) **Action Specific Exception Handling:**
   i) Define <exception> tag within <action> tag
   ii) Available to the particular action class
   iii) Useful when any custom JSP page needs to be displayed in case of exceptions

256: Write a code for action specific exceptions handler.

Answer:

```
<action-mappings>
    <action path="..." type="..." scope="..." name="..."
        validate="true" input="/addUser.jsp">
```

```
        <forward ... />
        <exception key="user.exception"
        type="com.ks.userException"
            path="/WEB-INF/userExcep.jsp" />
    </action>
</action-mappings>
```

257: How and where will you define global exceptions?

Answer:

a) Define global exceptions in struts-config.xml file
b) Available to the whole application (for all action classes)

```
<global-exceptions>
    <exception key="user.exception"
        type="com.ks.NoUserFoundException"
        path="/WEB-INF/jsp/userExcep.jsp" />
</global-exceptions>
```

258: What are the steps to create custom exception handler?

Answer:

a) Create custom exception handler class extending ExceptionHandler class
b) Define it in struts-config.xml using "handler" attribute in <exception> tag

```
<exception  key="user.exception"
    type="com.ks.NoUserFoundException"
    handler="com.ks.UserExceptionHandler"
    path="/WEB-INF/jsp/userExcep.jsp" />
```

259: How will you handle Http error 404 in struts?

Answer:

a) Using <error-page> tag in struts-config.xml file.
b) Give the error page path in <location> tag inside <error-page>.

```
<web-app>
    ...
    <servlet> .. </servlet>
    <servlet-mapping> ... </servlet-mapping>
    <error-page>
        <error-code>404</error-code>
        <location>/ks/errors/httpErrorCode.jsp </location>
    </error-page>
</web-app>
```

Chapter **32**

Validation and Validator Framework

260: What is Client-side validation and Server-side validation?

Answer:

a) **Client side validation:** Validation is done in client side using scripting (Struts uses Javascript) before submitting the form data to the server

Disadvantages:

i) Client may disable the browser scripting

ii) Not all browsers fully support Javascript

iii) Javascript cannot access server resources such as database

iv) Hackers can avoid client side validation

Advantage:

i) Save network bandwidth since validation is done in

client side which avoids roundtrip between client and server

b) **Server side validation:** Validation is done by the web application running on the server

Advantages:

i) Can access server resources such as database since the code is running in the server

ii) Requires web application to retrieve data from the request sent by the client. Hence hackers cannot do bypass this validation

Disadvantages:

i) Occupies more server CPU cycles because of communication between server and client for each validation

ii) Hence affects scalability

iii) Requires more network bandwidth to pass request to the server

iv) Requires some extra post-back to redisplay the page and display the error messages if validation fails

261: What are the methods in struts to validate the form data?

Answer:

The methods in struts to validate the form data are:

a) **Declarative validation:** Using Validator framework which uses two configuration files. (Client and Server side supported validation)

b) **Programmatic validation:** Using validate() method in Action Form bean and using execute() method in Action class (Server side validation)

262: What is the configuration required for using validate() method and post-back the error messages to the user form page?

Answer:

a) By setting "validate" attribute to "true" in the <action> tag within <action-mapping> in struts-config.xml file

b) Specify the jsp name in the "input" attribute which is the post-back location. Redisplaying the page with validation error messages is called post-back. That is, if the ActionErrors object that is populated in validate() method, is non-empty, the error messages will be displayed to this "input" jsp page. Error message will be present in application message properties file

```
<action-mappings>
    <action path="..." type="..." scope="..." name="..."
        validate="true" input="/addUser.jsp">
        <forward .../>
    </action>
</action-mappings>
```

263: How is the validate() method in the Action class better than validator framework?

Answer:

a) **Validator framework:** Client side validation which uses Javascript and it can be cracked through. Client browser must support scripting to make it work

b) **validate() method:** Server side validation and the code will reside in java form bean so that it cannot be cracked through

264: Explain about DynaValidatorForm.

Answer:

a) DynaValidatorForm extends from DynaActionForm which is used to define the form properties in the struts-config.xml file instead of creating separate ActionForm for each form bean
b) It provides XML based field validation
c) The "name" attribute of the form being provided in the struts-config.xml should match the form's "name" attribute in the validation.xml file

Struts-config.xml:

```
<form-beans>
    <form-bean name="UserForm"
        type="org.apache.struts.validator.DynaValidatorForm" >
      <form-property name="name" type="java.lang.String" />
      <form-property name="age" type="java.lang.Integer" />
    </form-bean>
</form-beans>
```

265: How is validation performed using validator framework in Struts?

Answer:

Validation performed using validator framework in Struts by:

a) Using Validator framework which consists of 2 files: validator.xml and validator-rules.xml

b) Create application message resource properties file to create error messages

c) With Client side validation enabled, if any error occurs, javascript will pop up a error message box, provided client browser needs to support scripting

Validation.xml:

```
<form-validation>
    <formset>
        <form name=" UserForm">
            <field  property="name"  depends="required">
                <arg  key="UserForm.name "/>
            </field>
            <field  property="age"  depends="required ">
                <arg  key="UserForm.age "/>
            </field>
        </form>
    </formset>
</form-validation>
```

266: What are the steps required for setting up validator framework in Struts?

Answer:

The steps required for setting up validator framework in Struts are:

a) Write validator.xml and validator-rules.xml files and place it under WEB-INF folder

b) Define ValidatorPlugIn in struts-config.xml

c) Write validation.xml file to define the user form bean

validation

d) Write ActionForm that extends ValidatorForm class
e) Define DynaValidatorForm class in struts-config.xml file
f) If more than one validation file is required, specify as comma delimited file list. Validation files will be checked one by one in the order they have been declared in ValidatorPlugIn

267: Explain about Validation.xml and validator-rules.xml files.

Answer:

a) **validator-rules.xml**
    i) Contains default validator definitions for all data types
    ii) Can add new entry in this file
    iii) Available in struts distribution library. It is not advisable to create this file ourself even though it is configurable
    iv) Defines JAVASCRIPT to be used for Client side validation
b) **Validation.xml**
    i) Used for different form beans
    ii) Can give different file name for the user defined validation

268: How will you configure Validator plugin in struts configuration file?

Answer:

We can configure Validator plugin in struts configuration file:

a) By defining ValidatorPlugIn class in the struts-config.xml file

b) Setting validation files location in the property "pathnames"

```
<plug-in
className="org.apache.struts.validator.ValidatorPlugIn">
<set-property property="pathnames"
    value="/WEB-INF/validator-rules.xml, /WEB-
    INF/validation.xml "/>
</plug-in>
```

269: Can we write user defined validation file and configure it in ValidatorPlugin?

Answer:

a) Yes. Write a user defined validation file as validation.xml
b) No naming convention and needs to be given along with the validation.xml files in ValidatorPlugin

```
<plug-in
className="org.apache.struts.validator.ValidatorPlugIn">
    <set-property  property="pathnames"
            value="/WEB-INF/validator-rules.xml, /WEB-
            INF/validation.xml,
        /WEB-INF/validation-processUser.xml "/>
</plug-in>
```

270: How will you display the validation errors in a jsp page?

Answer:

a) We can display the validation errors in a jsp page using <html:errors/> tag
b) Error messages or messages keys are stored in

ActionErrors object which will be then stored in request attribute using saveErrors() method as below

c) saveErrors(req, actionErrors)

271: How will you copy struts actionform contents to POJO/model class in order to save it database?

Answer:

a) We can copy struts actionform contents to POJO/model class in order to save it database using copyProperties() of BeanUtils
b) BeanUtils.copyProperties(user, userForm)
c) "user" – is Model/POJO class and "userForm" - struts ActionForm
d) Use the aforementioned statement within execute() method of action class

272: How will you do the front-end javascript validation by using Validator framework?

Answer:

a) Using <html:javascript> tag in jsp to create client side javascript validation
b) Ensure that the validator plugin is configured in struts-config.xml file
c) Create validation.xml file and application message properties file for form labels
d) Include below tag in the jsp after the form fields/properties within <html:form>
e) < html:javascript formName="userForm" />

Chapter **33**

Logic Tags

273: What are the various struts Tag libraries?

Answer:

The various struts tag libraries are:

a) **Bean tags:** To define new beans, access existing beans and its properties
b) **Html tags:** To create input forms, html based UI
Other tags such as <html:errors>, <html:messages>, <html:link>
c) **Logic tags:** To iterate over collections, conditional operations (comparison)
d) **Tiles tags:** To define layouts (header, body, footer etc), dynamic page building
e) **Nested tags:** To handle beans that hold references to other beans internally

274: How are the tag libraries defined in struts1.2?

Answer:

The tag libraries in struts1.2 are:

a) Defined in web.xml
b) The below configuration in web.xml file can be omitted by specifying URI as <%@ taglib uri="http://struts.apache.org/tags-tiles" prefix="tiles" %> from struts 1.3 onwards

<u>Web.xml file:</u>

```
<taglib>
    <taglib-uri>/WEB-INF/struts-bean.tld</taglib-uri>
    <taglib-location>/WEB-INF/struts-bean.tld</taglib-location>
</taglib>
```

275: How the drop down list is populated in struts using Form Properties?

Answer:

The drop down list is populated in struts using Form Properties using "html:options" tag and "property" & "labelProperty" attributes.

```
<html:select name="UserForm" property="user" multiple="true">
    <bean:define name="UserForm" property="userList"
    id="userColl" />
    <html:options collection="userColl " property="userID"
    labelProperty="userName" />
</html:select>
```

276: What are differences between <bean:message> and <bean:write>?

Answer:

a) **<bean:write>:** Used to read and write the bean property values.

b) **<bean:message>:** Used to display localize message from properties file.

```
<bean:message  key="user.name"/>
<bean:write  name="user"  property="uname"/>
```

277: What is the use of <logic:iterate>?

Answer:

<logic:iterate>? is:

a) Used to iterate over collection object of Primitive type and Object type

b) **Iterate primitive type:**

   i) <u>Test.java:</u>

   ```
   List<String> userNames = new ArrayList<String>();
   ```

   ii) <u>Test.jsp:</u>

   ```
   <logic:iterate name=" userNames " id="userNameld">
       User names : <bean:write name=" userNameld "/>
   </logic:iterate>
   ```

c) **Iterate Object type:**

   i) <u>Test.java:</u>

   ```
   List<User> userList = new ArrayList<User>();
   ```

   ii) <u>Test.jsp:</u>

   ```
   <logic:iterate name=" userList" id="userListld">
       User List :
   ```

```
        <bean:write name=" userListId "
        property="uname" />
        <bean:write name=" userListId " property="age" />
    </logic:iterate>
```

278: What library must be used if you want to use checkboxes, drop down list, text boxes?

Answer:

a) Using HTML tag library
b) Html form tags such as <html:submit>, <html:checkboxes> should be placed within <html:form> tag

279: How will you configure if you require navigating from standard index.jsp file to another jsp file (for instance, login page) to avoid implementing the application logic in index.jsp?

Answer:

a) **In index.jsp:** Use taglib directive and give URI for struts-logic tag.
```
<logic:redirect action="/userLogin.do"/>
```
b) **In struts-config.xml:** Use ForwardAction.
```
<action path="/userLogin"
    type="org.apache.struts.actions.ForwardAction"
    scope="request"
    parameter="/WEB-INF/jsp/login.jsp"/>
```

Chapter **34**

Internationalization / Localization

280: Explain how the resource bundles are used for Localization.

Answer:

Struts 2 uses the different resource bundles available to handle internationalization and localization. Instead of having the display text and messages in many languages which is stored in key-value pairs, you can create a resource bundle for each language to be supported. The resource bundles are searched in the order ActionClass.properties, Interface.properties, SuperClass.properties, model.properties, package.properties, struts.properties, and global.properties. For each country and language, a different global properties file will have to be created and maintained. For example, global.properties by default takes US English as the default language. For Spanish locale, global_es.properties and for French locale, global_fr.properties are required.

281: Explain the naming convention of a resource file in struts2.

Answer:

You can add resource bundles in the format *bundlename_language_country.properties*. ActionClass, SuperClass, Interface, Package, Model, and Global resource properties are the expected bundle names. The language_country part is the country locale for the particular country such as en_US for US English and es_ES for Spanish. The resource bundles always store data in key-value pairs. So if you are looking for global labels in French, your file must be global_fr_FR.properties where FR is for the country France which can be omitted. For locale specific package file, it should be saved as packageName.properties or packageName_fr_FR.properties. Similarly the ActionClass bundles must be saved as actionclassname.properties or actionclassname_fr_FR.properties. This has to be done for each language supported.

282: Name the interceptors responsible for Internationalization and Localization in Struts2

Answer:

The interceptor responsible for Internationalization in Struts 2 is the *I18nInterceptor*. You will see this configured in the struts-default.xml configuration file under *i18n*. When the *I18nInterceptor* receives a value for the *request_locale* it triggers checking for the corresponding resource bundle as per the locale. Since the

I18nInterceptor is a part of the default interceptor stack, nothing explicit has to be done for localization.

283: What are the steps to create Localization application?

Answer:

The steps to create Localization application are:

a) Write properties file for all localize messages. That is properties file contains the contents based on the specified language. File name will be "filename_lang_code.properties". For instance, "myprop_en_US.properties"

b) Write an Action class containing multiple methods for each language

c) Write an Action Form overriding validate () and reset ()methods

d) In JSP, Give the action path appropriately to display the web page in selected language

<html:link page="/mylocale1.do?method=langEng">

284: Where is the Locale attribute stored by the struts?

Answer:

a) In the user SessionContext under a key Globals.LOCALE_KEY, for each user

b) request.getSession().setAttribute (Globals.LOCALE_KEY, Locale.ENGLISH)

c) Package org.apache.struts.Globals

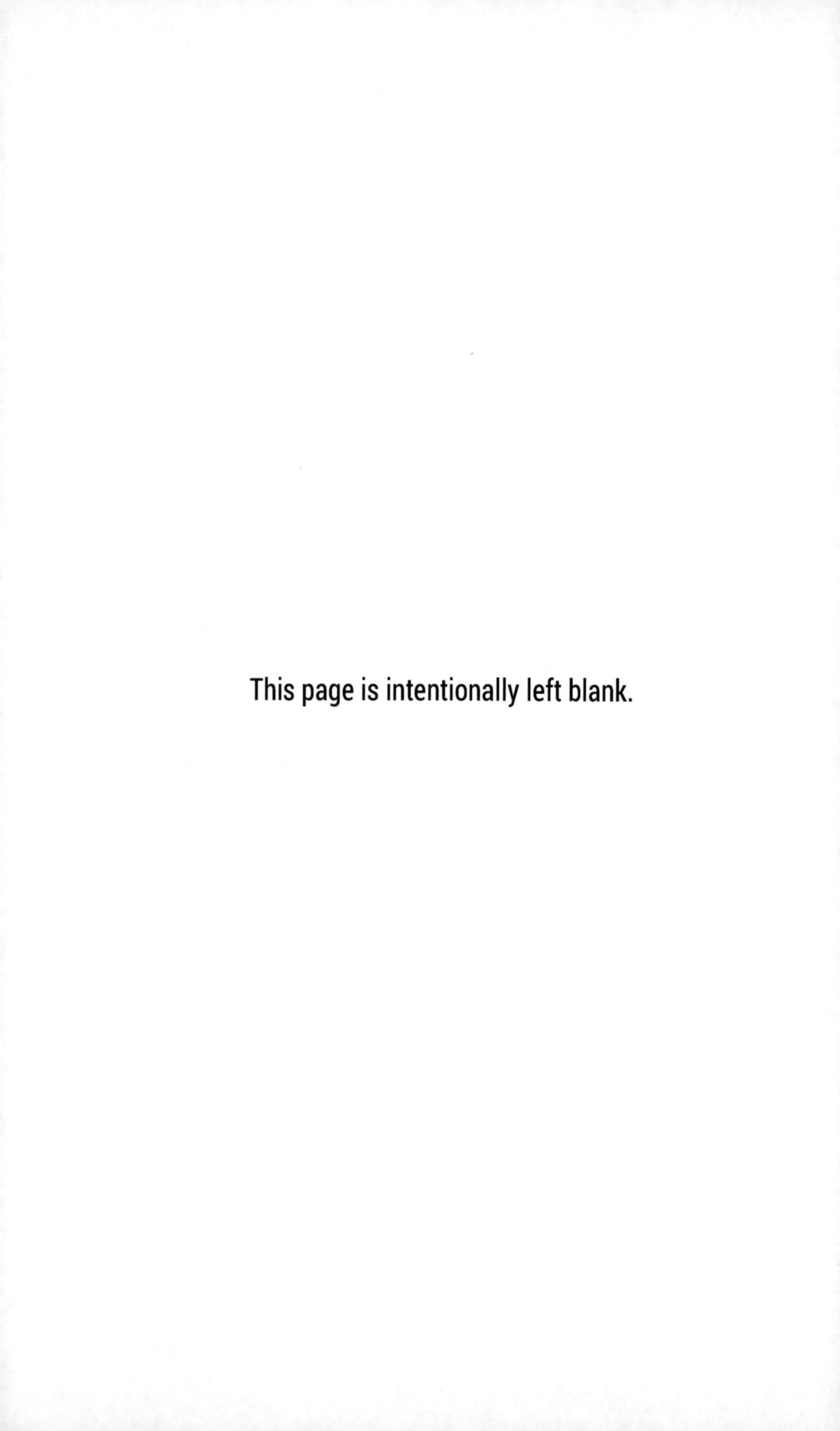
This page is intentionally left blank.

Chapter **35**

Integrate with other Frameworks

285: What are the steps to integrate struts with hibernate?

Answer:

The steps to integrate struts with hibernate are:

a) Write Struts-Hibernate plugin class/file that implements PlugIn interface
b) Store sessionFactory into servletContext using ActionServlet object
c) Define the plugin file in the struts configuration file
d) Retrieve the sessionFactory in Struts action class to do hibernate operations

286: How will you define the struts hibernate plugin file in the struts-config.xml file?

Answer:

The struts hibernate plugin file in the struts-config.xml file can be defined as follows:

```
<struts-config>
        ...
    <plug-in className=
    "com.ks.hibPlugins.StrutsHibernatePlugin">
        <set-property property="path" value="/hib.cfg.xml"/>
    </plug-in>
        ...
<struts-config>
```

287: How will you store Sessionfactory into ServletContext and retrieve the same?

Answer:

a) **Store using setAttribute():** myServlet1 of type ActionServlet

    mySservlet1.getServletContext().setAttribute (SF_KEY1, sessnFact);

b) **Retrieve using getAttribute():**

    SessionFactory sf = (SessionFactory)myServlet1.
    getServletContext()
        getAttribute (StrutsHibernatePlugin.SF_KEY1);

288: How will you define struts Tiles plugin?

Answer:

We can define struts tiles plugin as follows:

```
<plug-in className="org.apache.struts.tiles.TilesPlugin" >
    <set-property property="definitions-config"
```

```
        value="/WEB-INF/tilesDefinitions.xml" />
    <set-property  property="moduleAware" value="true" />
</plug-in>
```

289: How will you configure spring with struts?

Answer:

We can configure spring with struts using ContextLoaderPlugIn spring plugin with struts:

```
<plug-in className =
"org.springframework.web.struts.ContextLoaderPlugIn" >
    <set-property property="contextConfigLocation"
    value="/WEB-INF/spring.xml"/>
</plug-in>
```

290: How will you configure struts if the action class requires to be mapped with spring bean, for instance, if it requires any other bean injection?

Answer:

We can configure struts if the action class requires to be mapped with spring bean, for instance, if it requires any other bean injection as below:

a) Using DelegatingActionProxy, the control will be forwarded to spring ApplicationContext configuration file
b) Struts action "path" and spring bean should be same

Struts-config.xml:

```
    <action path="/user"
        type=
        "org.springframework.web.struts.DelegatingActionProxy"
        >
```

```
        <forward name="succ" path="/user.jsp"/>
    </action>
```

<u>Spring.xml:</u>

```
    <bean name="/user" class="...">
            ...
    </bean>
```

Chapter **36**

Action and ActionForms

291: What is the role of RequestProcessor in struts?

Answer:

a) RequestProcessor is used for processing the requests
b) If the request comes to the ActionServlet, it will invoke the process() method of RequestProcessor, which looks for the struts-config.xml and locates the action class path that has come along with the request
c) Once it identifies the action class, it will process the request

292: What is the difference between ActionForm and DynaActionForm?

Answer:

a) **ActionForm:**
   i) Need to create ActionForm class with Jsp form

properties and its getters/setters methods

ii) Properties are checked in compile time

iii) Properties of ActionForm can be accessed by JSTL EL directly

-${userForm.uname}

iv) To access ActionForm properties, copy it to another java bean class

b) DynaActionForm:

i) No need to create ActionForm class and the properties are declared in struts-config.xml file using <form-bean> and <form-property> tags

ii) Run time property checking

iii) Properties of DynaActionForm can be accessed by JSTL EL through slightly different syntax

-${userForm.map.uname

-HashMap is containing DynaActionForm properties

iv) Access properties using its getter method as userForm.get("uname") as it is a Map type

293: What is the difference between DispatchAction and LookupDispatchAction?

Answer:

a) **DispatchAction:**

i) Method name in the action class should be same as jsp form's button name

ii) Based on the "parameter" property value in <action> tag

iii) That is, based on the method name (of buttons)

   iv) Selects the method based on the "parameter" value configured in the <action> tag
   v) Not useful for I18N Internationalization
   vi) <html:submit property="crud">Add</html:submit>

b) **LookupDispatchAction:**
   i) Method name in the action class need not be same as jsp form's button name.
   ii) Based on the lookup for the key value (Map) in action class.
   iii) Looks up for the key name in the resource bundle.
   iv) Mapping of the method name and button name (key name) is done by overriding getKeyMethodMap().
   v) Useful for I18N Internationalization.
   vi) <html:submit property="crud">
   <bean:message key="user.add"/>
   </html:submit>

294: Explain LookupDispatchAction.

Answer:

LookupDispatchAction:

a) Extends from DispatchAction
b) Used to group related functions into single Action class
c) JSP button name need not be same as method names in action class
d) Mapping of button name and method name is done by defining getKeyMethodMap() in the action class
e) If duplicate key values exist in the map, it will take the first key value found

f) The "property" attribute of <html:submit> in jsp should be same as "parameter" attribute of <action> tag in struts-config.xml file

295: What is the use of Switch Action?

Answer:

a) Switch Action is used to switch from a resource in one module to another module's resource in the same application
b) Modular application is the one where multiple modules are working separately
c) For each modules separate struts-config.xml files can be used

```
<action  path="/module2"
     type="org.apache.struts.actions.SwitchAction" />
```

d) For instance, if 2 modules are used, aforementioned SwitchAction has to be included in both modules' configuration file
e) In <global-forwards>, switch action can be defined with action "path" for module

296: What are ActionErrors and ActionMessage?

Answer:

a) **ActionErrors**
   i) Encapsulates errors populated in the validate() method of ActionForm. Deprecated
   ii) Either global or specific to bean property
   iii) Saved by saveErrors() method

b) **ActionMessage**

   i) Encapsulates errors messages

   ii) Either global or specific to bean property

   iii) Saved by saveMessages() method

297: Explain about the Token feature in struts.

Answer:

a) Struts assign a token value for each form that is displayed, in a session object and maintains it in the form as a hidden property. If the form validation fails (invalid token), it means that the form is resubmitted

b) Used to avoid duplicate form submit. That is, clicking a submit button more than once (OR) Click the browser BACK button and submit the form again (OR) REFRESH the page and submit it

298: How will you handle duplicate form submission?

Answer:

Duplicate form submission can be handled as follows:

a) Using saveToken(request), isTokenValid(request), resetToken(request) methods

b) Invoke the saveToken(request) method from the Action class to create a new Token for the request and it is in turn stored into session object using Globals.TRANSACTION_TOKEN_KEY. "TOKEN" is the value of the key

c) Create a hidden form field in the jsp page to retrieve the token value

d) Before insert or update is performed in action class, call isTokenValid(request) method. If it fails, form is resubmitted

e) After insert or update, invoke resetToken(request) method without fail

299: Can we declare Instance variables in Action class and if yes, what will happen?

Answer:

a) No. It is not advisable to declare Instance variables in Action class

b) Since only one instance will be created for an action class and used by multiple threads (requests), all of them can share/modify the instance variable which is not synchronized

c) So it is advisable to declare variables inside the methods

d) However, Struts2 action class is thread-safe where new instance will be created for each request

300: How will you download a file from the server/website displaying saveas dialog box?

Answer:

We can download a file from the server/website displaying saveas dialog box as follows:

a) Include the below changes in the action class which will return/open save dialog box

b) Set the ContentType, Header of response object

```
resp.setContentType("application/octet-stream");
```

```
resp.setHeader("Content-Disposition",
"attachment;filename=ksfile1.zip");
```

c) Gets the file from the file system using FileInputStream

```
FileInputStream fis = new FileInputStream(new
File("C:\\ksfile1.zip"));
```

d) File that resides in web application path can be retrieved using getResource() method

```
URL ksurl2 =
getServlet().getServletContext().getResource("ks/ksfile
1.zip");

InputStream fis = ksurl2.openStream();
```

e) Create output stream using getOutputStream() method

```
ServletOutputStream sos = resp.getOutputStream();
```

f) Read the binary contents from input stream "fis" and copy to output stream as "sos.write(...)"

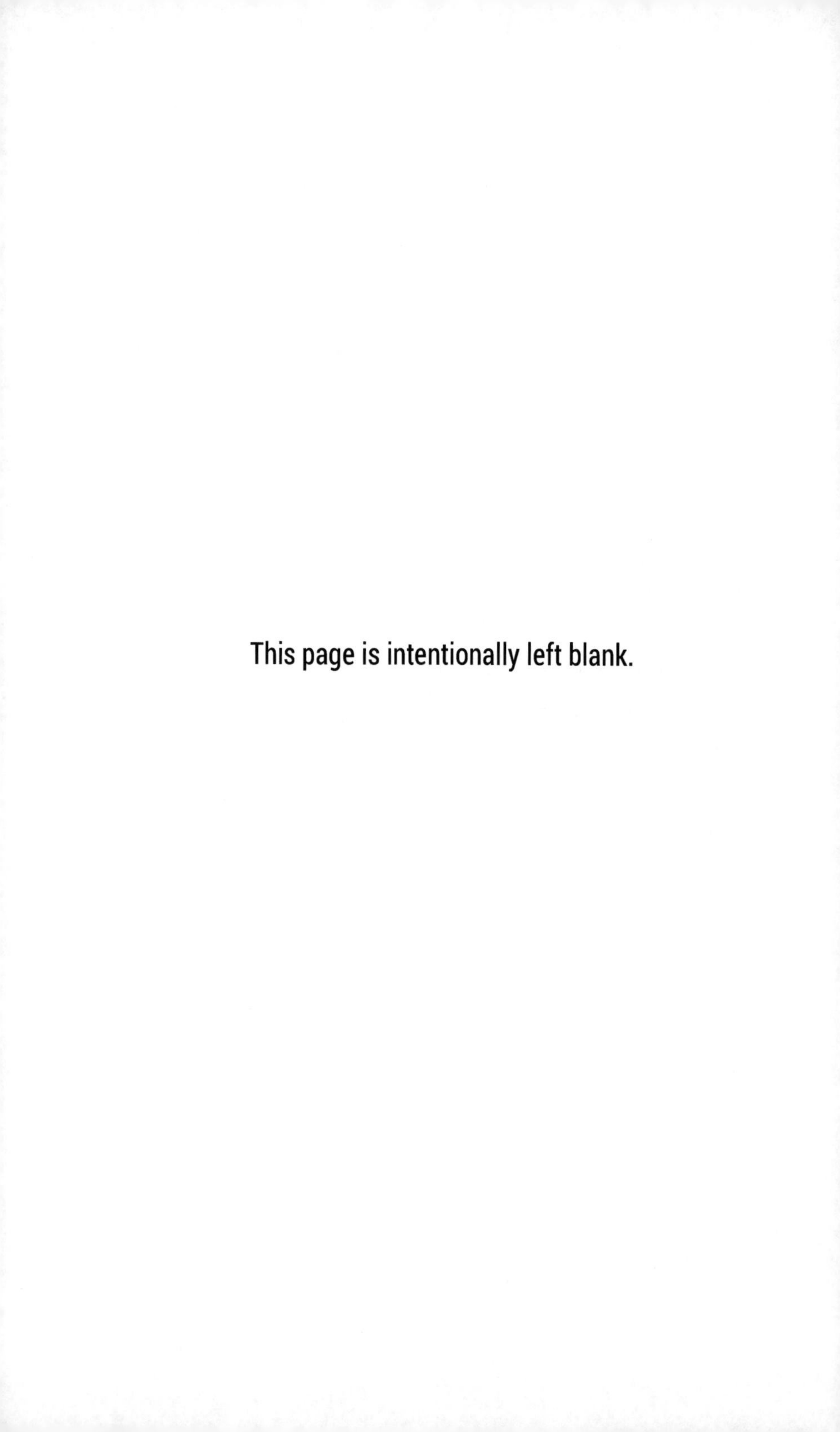
This page is intentionally left blank.

HR Questions

Review these typical interview questions and think about how you would answer them. Read the answers listed; you will find best possible answers along with strategies and suggestions.

1: Would you rather receive more authority or more responsibility at work?

Answer:

There are pros and cons to each of these options, and your interviewer will be more interested to see that you can provide a critical answer to the question. Receiving more authority may mean greater decision-making power and may be great for those with outstanding leadership skills, while greater responsibility may be a growth opportunity for those looking to advance steadily throughout their careers.

2: What do you do when someone in a group isn't contributing their fair share?

Answer:

This is a particularly important question if you're interviewing for a position in a supervisory role – explain the ways in which you would identify the problem, and how you would go about pulling aside the individual to discuss their contributions. It's important to understand the process of creating a dialogue, so that you can communicate your expectations clearly to the individual, give them a chance to respond, and to make clear what needs to change. After this, create an action plan with the group member to ensure their contributions are on par with others in the group.

3: Tell me about a time when you made a decision that was outside of your authority.

Answer:

While an answer to this question may portray you as being

decisive and confident, it could also identify you to an employer as a potential problem employee. Instead, it may be best to slightly refocus the question into an example of a time that you took on additional responsibilities, and thus had to make decisions that were outside of your normal authority (but which had been granted to you in the specific instance). Discuss how the weight of the decision affected your decision-making process, and the outcomes of the situation.

4: Are you comfortable going to supervisors with disputes?

Answer:

If a problem arises, employers want to know that you will handle it in a timely and appropriate manner. Emphasize that you've rarely had disputes with supervisors in the past, but if a situation were to arise, you feel perfectly comfortable in discussing it with the person in question in order to find a resolution that is satisfactory to both parties.

5: If you had been in charge at your last job, what would you have done differently?

Answer:

No matter how many ideas you have about how things could run better, or opinions on the management at your previous job, remain positive when answering this question. It's okay to show thoughtful reflection on how something could be handled in order to increase efficiency or improve sales, but be sure to keep all of your suggestions focused on making things better, rather than talking about ways to eliminate waste or negativity.

6: Do you believe employers should praise or reward employees for a job well done?

Answer:

Recognition is always great after completing a difficult job, but there are many employers who may ask this question as a way to infer as to whether or not you'll be a high-maintenance worker. While you may appreciate rewards or praise, it's important to convey to the interviewer that you don't require accolades to be confident that you've done your job well. If you are interviewing for a supervisory position where you would be the one praising other employees, highlight the importance of praise in boosting team morale.

7: What do you believe is the most important quality a leader can have?

Answer:

There are many important skills for a leader to have in any business, and the most important component of this question is that you explain why the quality you choose to highlight is important. Try to choose a quality such as communication skills, or an ability to inspire people, and relate it to a specific instance in which you displayed the quality among a team of people.

8: Tell me about a time when an unforeseen problem arose. How did you handle it?

Answer:

It's important that you are resourceful, and level-headed under pressure. An interviewer wants to see that you handle problems systematically, and that you can deal with change in an orderly process. Outline the situation clearly, including all solutions and results of the process you implemented.

9: Can you give me an example of a time when you were able to improve X objective at your previous job?

Answer:

It's important here to focus on an improvement you made that created tangible results for your company. Increasing efficiency is certainly a very important element in business, but employers are also looking for concrete results such as increased sales or cut expenses. Explain your process thoroughly, offering specific numbers and evidence wherever possible, particularly in outlining the results.

10: Tell me about a time when a supervisor did not provide specific enough direction on a project.

Answer:

While many employers want their employees to follow very specific guidelines without much decision-making power, it's important also to be able to pick up a project with vague direction and to perform self-sufficiently. Give examples of necessary questions that you asked, and specify how you determined whether a question was something you needed to ask of a supervisor or whether it was something you could determine on your own.

11: Tell me about a time when you were in charge of leading a

project.

Answer:

Lead the interviewer through the process of the project, just as you would have with any of your team members. Explain the goal of the project, the necessary steps, and how you delegated tasks to your team. Include the results, and what you learned as a result of the leadership opportunity.

12: Tell me about a suggestion you made to a former employer that was later implemented.

Answer:

Employers want to see that you're interested in improving your company and doing your part – offer a specific example of something you did to create a positive change in your previous job. Explain how you thought of the idea, how your supervisors received it, and what other employees thought was the idea was put into place.

13: Tell me about a time when you thought of a way something in the workplace could be done more efficiently.

Answer:

Focus on the positive aspects of your idea. It's important not to portray your old company or boss negatively, so don't elaborate on how inefficient a particular system was. Rather, explain a situation in which you saw an opportunity to increase productivity or to streamline a process, and explain in a general step-by-step how you implemented a better system.

14: Is there a difference between leading and managing people – which is your greater strength?

Answer:

There is a difference – leaders are often great idea people, passionate, charismatic, and with the ability to organize and inspire others, while managers are those who ensure a system runs, facilitate its operations, make authoritative decisions, and who take great responsibility for all aspects from overall success to the finest decisions. Consider which of these is most applicable to the position, and explain how you fit into this role, offering concrete examples of your past experience.

15: Do you function better in a leadership role, or as a worker on a team?

Answer:

It is important to consider what qualities the interviewer is looking for in your position, and to express how you embody this role. If you're a leader, highlight your great ideas, drive and passion, and ability to incite others around you to action. If you work great in teams, focus on your dedication to the task at hand, your cooperation and communication skills, and your ability to keep things running smoothly.

16: Tell me about a time when you discovered something in the workplace that was disrupting your (or others) productivity – what did you do about it?

Answer:

Try to not focus on negative aspects of your previous job too much, but instead choose an instance in which you found a positive, and quick, solution to increase productivity. Focus on the way you noticed the opportunity, how you presented a solution to your supervisor, and then how the change was implemented (most importantly, talk about how you led the change initiative). This is a great opportunity for you to display your problem-solving skills, as well as your resourceful nature and leadership skills.

17: How do you perform in a job with clearly-defined objectives and goals?

Answer:

It is important to consider the position when answering this question – clearly, it is best if you can excel in a job with clearly-defined objectives and goals (particularly if you're in an entry level or sales position). However, if you're applying for a position with a leadership role or creative aspect to it, be sure to focus on the ways that you additionally enjoy the challenges of developing and implementing your own ideas.

18: How do you perform in a job where you have great decision-making power?

Answer:

The interviewer wants to know that, if hired, you won't be the type of employee who needs constant supervision or who asks for advice, authority, or feedback every step of the way. Explain that you work well in a decisive, productive environment, and that you look forward to taking initiative in your position.

19: If you saw another employee doing something dishonest or unethical, what would you do?

Answer:

In the case of witnessing another employee doing something dishonest, it is always best to act in accordance with company policies for such a situation – and if you don't know what this company's specific policies are, feel free to simply state that you would handle it according to the policy and by reporting it to the appropriate persons in charge. If you are aware of the company's policies (such as if you are seeking a promotion within your own company), it is best to specifically outline your actions according to the policy.

20: Tell me about a time when you learned something on your own that later helped in your professional life.

Answer:

This question is important because it allows the interviewer to gain insight into your dedication to learning and advancement. Choose an example solely from your personal life, and provide a brief anecdote ending in the lesson you learned. Then, explain in a clear and thorough manner how this lesson has translated into a usable skill or practice in your position.

21: Tell me about a time when you developed a project idea at work.

Answer:

Choose a project idea that you developed that was typical of projects you might complete in the new position. Outline where your idea came from, the type of research you did to ensure its success and relevancy, steps that were included in the project, and the end results. Offer specific before and after statistics, to show its success.

22: Tell me about a time when you took a risk on a project.

Answer:

Whether the risk involved something as complex as taking on a major project with limited resources or time, or simply volunteering for a task that was outside your field of experience, show that you are willing to stretch out of your comfort zone and to try new things. Offer specific examples of why something you did was risky, and explain what you learned in the process – or how this prepared you for a job objective you later faced in your career.

23: What would you tell someone who was looking to get into this field?

Answer:

This question allows you to be the expert – and will show the interviewer that you have the knowledge and experience to go along with any training and education on your resume. Offer your knowledge as advice of unexpected things that someone entering the field may encounter, and be sure to end with positive advice such as the passion or dedication to the work that is required to truly succeed.

24: How would you handle a negative coworker?

Answer:

Everyone has to deal with negative coworkers – and the single best way to do so is to remain positive. You may try to build a relationship with the coworker or relate to them in some way, but even if your efforts are met with a cold shoulder, you must retain your positive attitude. Above all, stress that you would never allow a coworker's negativity to impact your own work or productivity.

25: What would you do if you witnessed a coworker surfing the web, reading a book, etc, wasting company time?

Answer:

The interviewer will want to see that you realize how detrimental it is for employees to waste company time, and that it is not something you take lightly. Explain the way you would adhere to company policy, whether that includes talking to the coworker yourself, reporting the behavior straight to a supervisor, or talking to someone in HR.

26: How do you handle competition among yourself and other employees?

Answer:

Healthy competition can be a great thing, and it is best to stay focused on the positive aspects of this here. Don't bring up conflict among yourself and other coworkers, and instead focus on the motivation to keep up with the great work of others, and the ways in which coworkers may be a great support network in helping to push you to new successes.

27: When is it okay to socialize with coworkers?

Answer:

This question has two extreme answers (all the time, or never), and your interviewer, in most cases, will want to see that you fall somewhere in the middle. It's important to establish solid relationships with your coworkers, but never at the expense of getting work done. Ideally, relationship-building can happen with exercises of teamwork and special projects, as well as in the break room.

28: Tell me about a time when a major change was made at your last job, and how you handled it.

Answer:

Provide a set-up for the situation including the old system, what the change was, how it was implemented, and the results of the change, and include how you felt about each step of the way. Be sure that your initial thoughts on the old system are neutral, and that your excitement level grows with each step of the new change, as an interviewer will be pleased to see your adaptability.

29: When delegating tasks, how do you choose which tasks go to which team members?

Answer:

The interviewer is looking to gain insight into your thought process with this question, so be sure to offer thorough reasoning behind your choice. Explain that you delegate tasks based on each individual's personal strengths, or that you look at how many other projects each person is working on at the time, in order to create the best fit possible.

30: Tell me about a time when you had to stand up for something you believed strongly about to coworkers or a supervisor.

Answer:

While it may be difficult to explain a situation of conflict to an interviewer, this is a great opportunity to display your passions and convictions, and your dedication to your beliefs. Explain not just the situation to the interviewer, but also elaborate on why it was so important to you to stand up for the issue, and how your coworker or supervisor responded to you afterward – were they more respectful? Unreceptive? Open-minded? Apologetic?

31: Tell me about a time when you helped someone finish their work, even though it wasn't "your job."

Answer:

Though you may be frustrated when required to pick up someone else's slack, it's important that you remain positive about lending a hand. The interviewer will be looking to see if you're a team player, and by helping someone else finish a task that he or she couldn't manage alone, you show both your willingness to help the team succeed, and your own competence.

32: What are the challenges of working on a team? How do you handle this?

Answer:

There are many obvious challenges to working on a team, such as handling different perspectives, navigating individual schedules, or accommodating difficult workers. It's best to focus on one challenge, such as individual team members missing deadlines or failing to keep commitments, and then offer a solution that clearly addresses the problem. For example, you could organize weekly status meetings for your team to discuss progress, or assign shorter deadlines in order to keep the long-term deadline on schedule.

33: Do you value diversity in the workplace?

Answer:

Diversity is important in the workplace in order to foster an environment that is accepting, equalizing, and full of different perspectives and backgrounds. Be sure to show your awareness of these issues, and stress the importance of learning from others' experiences.

34: How would you handle a situation in which a coworker was not accepting of someone else's diversity?

Answer:

Explain that it is important to adhere to company policies regarding diversity, and that you would talk to the relevant supervisors or management team. When it is appropriate, it could also be best to talk to the coworker in question about the benefits of alternate perspectives – if you can handle the situation yourself, it's best not to bring resolvable issues to management.

35: Are you rewarded more from working on a team, or

accomplishing a task on your own?

Answer:

It's best to show a balance between these two aspects – your employer wants to see that you're comfortable working on your own, and that you can complete tasks efficiently and well without assistance. However, it's also important for your employer to see that you can be a team player, and that you understand the value that multiple perspectives and efforts can bring to a project.

36: Tell me about a time when you worked additional hours to finish a project.

Answer:

It's important for your employer to see that you are dedicated to your work, and willing to put in extra hours when required or when a job calls for it. However, be careful when explaining why you were called to work additional hours – for instance, did you have to stay late because you set goals poorly earlier in the process? Or on a more positive note, were you working additional hours because a client requested for a deadline to be moved up on short notice? Stress your competence and willingness to give 110% every time.

37: Tell me about a time when your performance exceeded the duties and requirements of your job.

Answer:

If you're a great candidate for the position, this should be an easy question to answer – choose a time when you truly went above and beyond the call of duty, and put in additional work or voluntarily took on new responsib-ilities. Remain humble, and express gratitude for the learning opportunity, as well as confidence in your ability to give a repeat performance.

38: What is your driving attitude about work?

Answer:

There are many possible good answers to this question, and the interviewer primarily wants to see that you have a great passion for the job and that you will remain motivated in your career if hired. Some specific driving forces behind your success may include hard work, opportunity, growth potential, or success.

39: Do you take work home with you?

Answer:

It is important to first clarify that you are always willing to take work home when necessary, but you want to emphasize as well that it has not been an issue for you in the past. Highlight skills such as time management, goal-setting, and multi-tasking, which can all ensure that work is completed at work.

40: Describe a typical work day to me.

Answer:

There are several important components in your typical work day, and an interviewer may derive meaning from any or all of them, as well as from your ability to systematically lead him or her through the day. Start at the beginning of your day and proceed chronologically, making sure to emphasize steady productivity, time for review, goal-setting, and prioritizing, as well as some additional time to account for unexpected things that may arise.

41: Tell me about a time when you went out of your way at your previous job.

Answer:

Here it is best to use a specific example of the situation that required you to go out of your way, what your specific position would have required that you did, and how you went above that. Use concrete details, and be sure to include the results, as well as reflection on what you learned in the process.

42: Are you open to receiving feedback and criticisms on your job performance, and adjusting as necessary?

Answer:

This question has a pretty clear answer – yes – but you'll need to display a knowledge as to why this is important. Receiving feedback and criticism is one thing, but the most important part of that process is to then implement it into your daily work. Keep a good attitude, and express that you always appreciate constructive feedback.

43: What inspires you?

Answer:

You may find inspiration in nature, reading success stories, or mastering a difficult task, but it's important that your inspiration is positively-based and that you're able to listen and tune into it when it appears. Keep this answer generally based in the professional world, but where applicable, it may stretch a bit into creative exercises in your personal life that, in turn, help you in achieving career objectives.

44: How do you inspire others?

Answer:

This may be a difficult question, as it is often hard to discern the effects of inspiration in others. Instead of offering a specific example of a time when you inspired someone, focus on general principles such as leading by example that you employ in your professional life. If possible, relate this to a quality that someone who inspired you possessed, and discuss the way you have modified or modeled it in your own work.

45: How do you make decisions?

Answer:

This is a great opportunity for you to wow your interviewer with your decisiveness, confidence, and organizational skills. Make sure that you outline a process for decision-making, and that you stress the importance of weighing your options, as well as in trusting intuition. If you answer this question skillfully and with ease, your interviewer will trust in your capability as a worker.

46: What are the most difficult decisions for you to make?

Answer:

Explain your relationship to decision-making, and a general synopsis of the process you take in making choices. If there is a particular type of decision that you often struggle with, such as those that involve other people, make sure to explain why that type of decision is tough for you, and how you are currently engaged in improving your skills.

47: When making a tough decision, how do you gather information?

Answer:

If you're making a tough choice, it's best to gather information from as many sources as possible. Lead the interviewer through your process of taking information from people in different areas, starting first with advice from experts in your field, feedback from coworkers or other clients, and by looking analytically at your own past experiences.

48: Tell me about a decision you made that did not turn out well.

Answer:

Honesty and transparency are great values that your interviewer will appreciate – outline the choice you made, why you made it, the results of your poor decision – and finally (and most importantly!) what you learned from the decision. Give the interviewer reason to trust that you wouldn't make a decision like that again in the future.

49: Are you able to make decisions quickly?

Answer:

You may be able to make decisions quickly, but be sure to communicate your skill in making sound, thorough decisions as well. Discuss the importance of making a decision quickly, and how you do so, as well as the necessity for each decision to first be well-informed.

50: What are the three most important things you're looking for in a position?

Answer:

The top three things you want in a position should be similar to the top three things the employer wants from an employee, so that it is clear that you are well-matched to the job. For example, the employer wants a candidate who is well-qualified for and has practical experience – and you want a position that allows you to use your education and skills to their best applications. The employer wants a candidate who is willing to take on new challenges and develop new systems to increase sales or productivity – and you want a position that pushes you and offers opportunities to develop, create, and lead new initiatives. The employer wants a candidate who will grow into and stay with the company for a long time – and you want a position that offers stability and believes in building a strong team. Research what the employer is looking for beforehand, and match your objectives to theirs.

51: How are you evaluating the companies you're looking to work with?

Answer:

While you may feel uncomfortable exerting your own requirements during the interview, the employer wants to see that you are thinking critically about the companies you're applying with, just as they are critically looking at you. Don't be afraid to specify what your needs from a company are (but do try to make sure they match up well with the company – preferably before you apply there), and show confidence and decisiveness in your answer. The interviewer wants to know that you're the kind of person who knows what they want, and how to get it.

52: Are you comfortable working for _________ salary?

Answer:

If the answer to this question is no, it may be a bit of a deal-breaker in a first interview, as you are unlikely to have much room to negotiate. You can try to leverage a bit by highlighting specific experience you have, and how that makes you qualified for more, but be aware that this is very difficult to navigate at this step of the process. To avoid this situation, be aware of industry standards and, if possible, company standards, prior to your application.

53: Why did you choose your last job?

Answer:

In learning what led you to your last job, the interviewer is able to get a feel for the types of things that motivate you. Keep these professionally-focused, and remain passionate about the early points of your career, and how excited you were to get started in the field.

54: How long has it been since your last job and why?

Answer:

Be sure to have an explanation prepared for all gaps in

employment, and make sure it's a professional reason. Don't mention difficulties you may have had in finding a job, and instead focus on positive things such as pursuing outside interests or perhaps returning to school for additional education.

55: What other types of jobs have you been looking for?

Answer:

The answer to this question can show the interviewer that you're both on the market and in demand. Mention jobs you've applied for or looked at that are closely related to your field, or similar to the position you're interviewing for. Don't bring up last-ditch efforts that found you applying for a part-time job completely unrelated to your field.

56: Have you ever been disciplined at work?

Answer:

Hopefully the answer here is no – but if you have been disciplined for something at work though, be absolutely sure that you can explain it thoroughly. Detail what you learned from the situation, and reflect on how you grew after the process.

57: What is your availability like?

Answer:

Your availability should obviously be as open as possible, and any gaps in availability should be explained and accounted for. Avoid asking about vacation or personal days (as well as other benefits), and convey to the interviewer how serious you are about your work.

58: May I contact your current employer?

Answer:

If possible, it is best to allow an interviewer to contact your current employer as a reference. However, if it's important that your employer is not contacted, explain your reason tactfully, such as you just started job searching and you haven't had the opportunity yet to inform them that you are looking for other employment. Be careful of this reasoning though, as employers may wonder if you'll start shopping for something better while employed with them as well.

59: Do you have any valuable contacts you could bring to our business?

Answer:

It's great if you can bring knowledge, references, or other contacts that your new employer may be able to network with. However, be sure that you aren't offering up any of your previous employer's clients, or in any way violating contractual agreements.

60: How soon would you be available to start working?

Answer:

While you want to be sure that you're available to start as soon as possible if the company is interested in hiring you, if you still have another job, be sure to give them at least two weeks' notice. Though your new employer may be anxious for you to start, they will want to hire a worker whom they can respect for giving adequate notice, so that they won't have to worry if you'll eventually leave them in the lurch.

61: Why would your last employer say that you left?

Answer:

The key to this question is that your employer's answer must be the same as your own answer about why you left. For instance, if you've told your employer that you left to find a position with greater opportunities for career advancement, your employer had better not say that you were let go for missing too many days of work. Honesty is key in your job application process.

62: How long have you been actively looking for a job?

Answer:

It's best if you haven't been actively looking for a job for very long, as a long period of time may make the interviewer wonder why no one else has hired you. If it has been awhile, make sure to explain why, and keep it positive. Perhaps you haven't come across many opportunities that provide you with enough of a challenge or that are adequately matched to someone of your education and experience.

63: When don't you show up to work?

Answer:

Clearly, the only time acceptable to miss work is for a real emergency or when you're truly sick – so don't start bringing up times now that you plan to miss work due to vacations or family birthdays. Alternatively, you can tell the interviewer how dedicated to your work you are, and how you always strive to be fully present and to put in the same amount of work every time you come in, even when you're feeling slightly under the weather.

64: What is the most common reason you miss work?

Answer:

If there is a reason that you will miss work routinely, this is the time to disclose it – but doing so during an interview will reflect negatively on you. Ideally, you will only miss work during cases of extreme illness or other emergencies.

65: What is your attendance record like?

Answer:

Be sure to answer this question honestly, but ideally you will have already put in the work to back up the fact that you rarely miss days or arrive late. However, if there are gaps in your attendance, explain them briefly with appropriate reasons, and make sure to emphasize your dedication to your work, and reliability.

66: Where did you hear about this position?

Answer:

This may seem like a simple question, but the answer can actually speak volumes about you. If you were referred by a friend or another employee who works for the company, this is a great chance to mention your connection (if the person is in good standing!). However, if you heard about it from somewhere like a career fair or a work placement agency, you may want to focus on how pleased you were to come across such a wonderful opportunity.

67: Tell me anything else you'd like me to know when making a hiring decision.

Answer:

This is a great opportunity for you to give a final sell of yourself to the interviewer – use this time to remind the interviewer of why you are qualified for the position, and what you can bring to the company that no one else can. Express your excitement for the opportunity to work with a company pursuing X mission.

68: Why would your skills be a good match with X objective of our company?

Answer:

If you've researched the company before the interview, answering this question should be no problem. Determine several of the company's main objectives, and explain how specific skills that you have are conducive to them. Also, think about ways that your experience and skills can translate to helping the company expand upon these objectives, and to reach further goals. If your old company had a similar objective, give a specific example of how you helped the company to meet it.

69: What do you think this job entails?

Answer:

Make sure you've researched the position well before heading into the interview. Read any and all job descriptions you can find (at best, directly from the employer's website or job posting), and make note of key duties, responsibilities, and experience required. Few things are less impressive to an interviewer than a candidate who has no idea what sort of job they're actually being interviewed for.

70: Is there anything else about the job or company you'd like to know?

Answer:

If you have learned about the company beforehand, this is a great opportunity to show that you put in the effort to study before the interview. Ask questions about the company's mission in relation to current industry trends, and engage the interviewer in interesting, relevant conversation. Additionally, clear up anything else you need to know about the specific position before leaving – so that if the interviewer calls with an offer, you'll be prepared to answer.

71: Are you the best candidate for this position?

Answer:

Yes! Offer specific details about what makes you qualified for this position, and be sure to discuss (and show) your unbridled passion and enthusiasm for the new opportunity, the job, and the company.

72: How did you prepare for this interview?

Answer:

The key part of this question is to make sure that you have prepared! Be sure that you've researched the company, their objectives, and their services prior to the interview, and know as much about the specific position as you possibly can. It's also helpful to learn about the company's history and key players in the current organization.

73: If you were hired here, what would you do on your first day?
Answer:

While many people will answer this question in a boring fashion, going through the standard first day procedures, this question is actually a great chance for you to show the interviewer why you will make a great hire. In addition to things like going through training or orientation, emphasize how much you would enjoy meeting your supervisors and coworkers, or how you would spend a lot of the day asking questions and taking in all of your new surroundings.

74: Have you viewed our company's website?
Answer:

Clearly, you should have viewed the company's website and done some preliminary research on them before coming to the interview. If for some reason you did not, do not say that you did, as the interviewer may reveal you by asking a specific question about it. If you did look at the company's website, this is an appropriate time to bring up something you saw there that was of particular interest to you, or a value that you especially supported.

75: How does X experience on your resume relate to this position?
Answer:

Many applicants will have some bit of experience on their resume that does not clearly translate to the specific job in question. However, be prepared to be asked about this type of seemingly-irrelevant experience, and have a response prepared that takes into account similar skill sets or training that the two may share.

76: Why do you want this position?

Answer:

Keep this answer focused positively on aspects of this specific job that will allow you to further your skills, offer new experience, or that will be an opportunity for you to do something that you particularly enjoy. Don't tell the interviewer that you've been looking for a job for a long time, or that the pay is very appealing, or you will appear unmotivated and opportunistic.

77: How is your background relevant to this position?

Answer:

Ideally, this should be obvious from your resume. However, in instances where your experience is more loosely-related to the position, make sure that you've researched the job and company well before the interview. That way, you can intelligently relate the experience and skills that you do have, to similar skills that would be needed in the new position. Explain specifically how your skills will translate, and use words to describe your background such as "preparation" and "learning." Your prospective position should be described as an "opportunity" and a chance for "growth and development."

78: How do you feel about X mission of our company?

Answer:

It's important to have researched the company prior to the interview – and if you've done so, this question won't catch you off guard. The best answer is one that is simple, to the point, and shows knowledge of the mission at hand. Offer a few short statements as to why you believe in the mission's importance, and note that you would be interested in the chance to work with a company that supports it.

And Finally Good Luck!

INDEX

Hibernate, Spring and Struts Interview Questions

Hibernate

Hibernate Interfaces

Hibernate Configuration

14: What is the flow of hibernate communication with database?

15: How will you configure Sequence generated primary key?

16: How will you change one relational database to another database without code changes?

17: What is dynamic-insert and dynamic-update option in the class mapping?

18: How will you configure Hibernate to access the instance variables directly without using setter method?

19: What is Automatic Dirty checking in hibernate?

20: Write down a sample code for Automatic Dirty checking.

21: How hibernate is database independent and what are the changes required?

22: How will you include hibernate mapping file in the hibernate configuration file?

Criteria Queries

23: What are the ways in which object can be fetched from the database in hibernate?

24: What is the use of Restrictions class?

25: How will you write criteria query to retrieve records having dept_name containing "hr" and emp_salary between 20000 and 30000?

26: How will you sort the employee class in descending order by employee salary using Criteria query?

27: How will you find out the maximum salary from Employee class?

28: What are the methods available in Projections class?

29: How will you implement pagination using criteria query?

30: What are the disadvantages of Criteria query?

31: How is the Primary Key created using Hibernate?

32: How do you create hibernate generated Primary Key?

Persistent Classes

Object States

O/R Mapping

53: Explain the different ORM levels.

54: What are the types of mapping?

55: Explain lazy loading in hibernate

56: What are the fetching strategies?

57: List out the Cascading options available in hibernate.

58: How will you enable cascading?

59: Explain about inverse attribute.

60: What is component mapping?

61: How do you make a class and collection as mutable in Hibernate mapping file?

62: What are the functions by which the entities are loaded and made read-only automatically, if Session.isDefaultReadOnly() method returns true?

63: What is the default access mode of immutable classes in hibernate and how will you change it?

64: Explain about mutable class in hibernate.

65: Explain about mutable collection in hibernate mapping file.

Hibernate Inheritance

66: Explain the advantages and disadvantages of implementing inheritance using Single Table Strategy.

67: Explain the advantages and disadvantages of implementing inheritance using With Table Per Class Strategy.

68: Explain the advantages and disadvantages of implementing inheritance using With Joined Strategy.

69: What are the types of Inheritance models? Explain.

70: What is unidirectional and bi-directional association in hibernate mapping?

Hibernate Caches

Hibernate Interceptor and Filters

operation of session, without having code duplication?

93: What is the use of Hibernate Filter?

94: Where will you define Filter and how?

95: How will you enable or disable hibernate Filter?

Spring

Spring Modules

96: What are the modules available in Spring Core Container Module?

97: What are the modules available in Spring Data Access / Integration Module?

98: What are the modules available in Spring Web Module?

99: What are the modules in Spring Framework?

IoC Container

100: Explain the 2 types of IoC containers.

101: Which is a better practice to follow – constructor based or setter based DI?

102: What is meant by IoC and DI?

103: What is the use of Spring Container?

Beans

104: Explain the Lifecycle of a Spring Bean.

105: What is meant by Beans in Spring?

106: How would you instantiate the container?

107: What is the difference between bean id and name attribute?

108: How will you achieve Factory design pattern in spring for Bean Creation?

Dependency Injection

Importing XML Resource

Idref Element

Bean Collaborators

126: Can I reference a bean defined in the parent container of the current bean? Explain

127: What are the advantages of using bean collaborators?

128: What is the difference between "local" and "bean" attribute of <ref> tag?

129: Explain about "parent" attribute of <ref> tag.

Collections

130: Explain the code for using a List collection in Spring.

131: Explain the code for using a Map collection in Spring.

132: Explain the code for using a Properties collection in Spring.

133: What are the types of collections that are supported by Spring?

134: How will you append the parent class properties with the child properties?

135: How will you assign "null" and " " empty string to the bean arguments?

Depends-on Attribute

136: What is the Depends-on Attribute used for?

137: Can you add a bean that depends on a singleton bean? Explain.

138: Write a simple example using depends-on attribute.

139: How will you specify the bean dependency explicitly?

140: Which bean will be destroyed first if "depends-on" attribute is used to define bean dependencies?

Lazy Initialized Bean

141: What is the advantage of Lazy initialization?

142: Analyze the following piece of code from a bean configuration. Explain how it affects the initialization of the bean.

143: How will you prevent the pre-instantiation of a singleton bean?

Autowiring

Bean Scopes

Bean Lifecycle Methods

Initialization Callbacks

Destruction Callbacks

Annotation Callbacks

160: What are the annotations used for the beans to accomplish certain tasks upon initialization and destruction?

161: What are the options available for controlling bean lifecycle behavior?

162: What is the execution order for bean Initialization if multiple lifecycle mechanisms are configured for the same bean?

163: What is the execution order for bean Destruction if multiple lifecycle mechanisms are configured for the same bean?

164: Is it possible for a bean object to define its own lifecycle methods/requirements.

Inheritance (Normal Inheritance)

165: How do you create an inheritance template?

166: Explain how to create an Abstract Bean and what is its use?

167: What is a pure inheritance template?

168: How will you implement inheritance in Spring?

Inheritance with Abstract

169: How will you prevent the base class from being instantiated?

170: Explain about Inheritance with Abstract attribute.

171: What will happen if you try to instantiate a bean that is declared as abstract in xml file?

172: How will you override base class property in subclass through Xml configuration file?

173: How will you define the bean's property value into a separate file instead of configuration XML file?

Annotations Based Configuration

174: Give an example of some annotations being supported by different versions of Sprin

ApplicationContext

Spring and Hibernate Integration

Spring AOP

192: What are the terminologies used in AOP?

193: What is AOP?

194: What is meant by Aspects?

195: Explain about Advice.

196: What is Join point and Pointcut?

197: How will you define aop "advice" when the bean name of PlatformTransactionManager is given with some other name instead of "transactionManager"?

198: How will you define pointcut and advisor if you want to execute the advice before executing any of the methods from a class/an interface?

199: How will make your advice to execute certain methods, for instance, starting with "get" in read-only transaction?

200: How will you rollback the declarative transaction using aop?

201: How will you enable annotation transaction management in spring AOP?

202: Give some examples of Spring AOP.

203: What are the types of Advice?

204: How will you implement Around Advice?

205: How do you implement AOP Proxy?

206: What is Advisor in AOP?

207: How will you implement Advisor?

208: How will you define pointcut and advice into single bean?

209: What will you do if you want to apply advice to the pointcut method which contains the word "dao" with the method name?

210: How will you avoid creating many proxy factory beans in spring AOP?

Struts

Configuration

Main Classes (Action classes and ActionForms)

233: How will you retrieve the values from JSP page if DynaActionForm is used?

234 How will you add multiple Application messages .properties file in struts-config.xml?

235: What will happen if name attribute of the <forward> in <action> tag is same as <global-forward> tag's <forward> name?

236: Write down a code for validate() and reset() methods.

237: Which method is used to execute the business logic in struts application?

238: What are the steps to write more than one related methods into single action class. For instance, to group the related methods such as add, update, delete into single action class?

239: Can we have parameterized constructor in ActionForm bean class?

240: How many instances will be created for an Action class in struts? Is action class thread-safe?

241: What is DynaActionForm and explain the steps to use it?

242: Can I have html form property without associating it with setters/getters methods of formbean?

243: Compare Struts1.0 and struts 1.1.

244: How many ActionServlets are created in struts application?

245: Why ActionServlet is singleton in Struts? Explain.

246: How does the container know whether it is a struts or spring application?

247: Explain about validate() and reset () methods.

248: Explain <global-forwards>.

249: What is the use of ForwardAction class?

250: What is the difference between ForwardAction and IncludeAction?

Exception Handling

251: How is exception handling simplified in Struts?

252: Explain Specific and Generic Exception handling in Struts 2?

Validation and Validator Framework

Logic Tags

274: How are the tag libraries defined in struts1.2?

275: How the drop down list is populated in struts using Form Properties?

276: What are differences between <bean:message> and <bean:write>?

277: What is the use of <logic:iterate>?

278: What library must be used if you want to use checkboxes, drop down list, text boxes?

279: How will you configure if you require navigating from standard index.jsp file to another jsp file (for instance, login page) to avoid implementing the application logic in index.jsp?

Internationalization / Localization

280: Explain how the resource bundles are used for Localization.

281: Explain the naming convention of a resource file in struts2.

282: Name the interceptors responsible for Internationalization and Localization in Struts2

283: What are the steps to create Localization application?

284: Where is the Locale attribute stored by the struts?

Integrate with other Frameworks

285: What are the steps to integrate struts with hibernate?

286: How will you define the struts hibernate plugin file in the struts-config.xml file?

287: How will you store Sessionfactory into ServletContext and retrieve the same?

288: How will you define struts Tiles plugin?

289: How will you configure spring with struts?

290: How will you configure struts if the action class requires to be mapped with spring bean, for instance, if it requires any other bean injection?

Action and ActionForms

HR Questions

1: Would you rather receive more authority or more responsibility at work?

2: What do you do when someone in a group isn't contributing their fair share?

3: Tell me about a time when you made a decision that was outside of your authority.

4: Are you comfortable going to supervisors with disputes?

5: If you had been in charge at your last job, what would you have done differently?

6: Do you believe employers should praise or reward employees for a job well done?

7: What do you believe is the most important quality a leader can have?

8: Tell me about a time when an unforeseen problem arose. How did you handle it?

9: Can you give me an example of a time when you were able to improve *X objective* at your previous job?

10: Tell me about a time when a supervisor did not provide specific enough direction on a project.

11: Tell me about a time when you were in charge of leading a project.

12: Tell me about a suggestion you made to a former employer that was later implemented.

13: Tell me about a time when you thought of a way something in the workplace could be done more efficiently.

14: Is there a difference between leading and managing people – which is your greater strength?

15: Do you function better in a leadership role, or as a worker on a team?

16: Tell me about a time when you discovered something in the workplace that was disrupting your (or others) productivity – what did you do about it?

17: How do you perform in a job with clearly-defined objectives and

36: Tell me about a time when you worked additional hours to finish a project.

37: Tell me about a time when your performance exceeded the duties and requirements of your job.

38: What is your driving attitude about work?

39: Do you take work home with you?

40: Describe a typical work day to me.

41: Tell me about a time when you went out of your way at your previous job.

42: Are you open to receiving feedback and criticisms on your job performance, and adjusting as necessary?

43: What inspires you?

44: How do you inspire others?

45: How do you make decisions?

46: What are the most difficult decisions for you to make?

47: When making a tough decision, how do you gather information?

48: Tell me about a decision you made that did not turn out well.

49: Are you able to make decisions quickly?

50: What are the three most important things you're looking for in a position?

51: How are you evaluating the companies you're looking to work with?

52: Are you comfortable working for __________ salary?

53: Why did you choose your last job?

54: How long has it been since your last job and why?

55: What other types of jobs have you been looking for?

56: Have you ever been disciplined at work?

57: What is your availability like?

58: May I contact your current employer?

59: Do you have any valuable contacts you could bring to our business?

60: How soon would you be available to start working?

61: Why would your last employer say that you left?

Some of the following titles might also be handy:

1. .NET Interview Questions You'll Most Likely Be Asked
2. 200 Interview Questions You'll Most Likely Be Asked
3. Access VBA Programming Interview Questions You'll Most Likely Be Asked
4. Adobe ColdFusion Interview Questions You'll Most Likely Be Asked
5. Advanced Excel Interview Questions You'll Most Likely Be Asked
6. Advanced JAVA Interview Questions You'll Most Likely Be Asked
7. Advanced SAS Interview Questions You'll Most Likely Be Asked
8. AJAX Interview Questions You'll Most Likely Be Asked
9. Algorithms Interview Questions You'll Most Likely Be Asked
10. Android Development Interview Questions You'll Most Likely Be Asked
11. Ant & Maven Interview Questions You'll Most Likely Be Asked
12. Apache Web Server Interview Questions You'll Most Likely Be Asked
13. Artificial Intelligence Interview Questions You'll Most Likely Be Asked
14. ASP.NET Interview Questions You'll Most Likely Be Asked
15. Automated Software Testing Interview Questions You'll Most Likely Be Asked
16. Base SAS Interview Questions You'll Most Likely Be Asked
17. BEA WebLogic Server Interview Questions You'll Most Likely Be Asked
18. C & C++ Interview Questions You'll Most Likely Be Asked
19. C# Interview Questions You'll Most Likely Be Asked
20. C++ Internals Interview Questions You'll Most Likely Be Asked
21. CCNA Interview Questions You'll Most Likely Be Asked
22. Cloud Computing Interview Questions You'll Most Likely Be Asked
23. Computer Architecture Interview Questions You'll Most Likely Be Asked
24. Computer Networks Interview Questions You'll Most Likely Be Asked
25. Core JAVA Interview Questions You'll Most Likely Be Asked
26. Data Structures & Algorithms Interview Questions You'll Most Likely Be Asked
27. Data WareHousing Interview Questions You'll Most Likely Be Asked
28. EJB 3.0 Interview Questions You'll Most Likely Be Asked
29. Entity Framework Interview Questions You'll Most Likely Be Asked
30. Fedora & RHEL Interview Questions You'll Most Likely Be Asked
31. GNU Development Interview Questions You'll Most Likely Be Asked
32. Hibernate, Spring & Struts Interview Questions You'll Most Likely Be Asked
33. HTML, XHTML and CSS Interview Questions You'll Most Likely Be Asked
34. HTML5 Interview Questions You'll Most Likely Be Asked
35. IBM WebSphere Application Server Interview Questions You'll Most Likely Be Asked
36. iOS SDK Interview Questions You'll Most Likely Be Asked
37. Java / J2EE Design Patterns Interview Questions You'll Most Likely Be Asked
38. Java / J2EE Interview Questions You'll Most Likely Be Asked
39. Java Messaging Service Interview Questions You'll Most Likely Be Asked
40. JavaScript Interview Questions You'll Most Likely Be Asked
41. JavaServer Faces Interview Questions You'll Most Likely Be Asked
42. JDBC Interview Questions You'll Most Likely Be Asked
43. jQuery Interview Questions You'll Most Likely Be Asked
44. JSP-Servlet Interview Questions You'll Most Likely Be Asked
45. JUnit Interview Questions You'll Most Likely Be Asked
46. Linux Commands Interview Questions You'll Most Likely Be Asked
47. Linux Interview Questions You'll Most Likely Be Asked
48. Linux System Administrator Interview Questions You'll Most Likely Be Asked
49. Mac OS X Lion Interview Questions You'll Most Likely Be Asked
50. Mac OS X Snow Leopard Interview Questions You'll Most Likely Be Asked

51. Microsoft Access Interview Questions You'll Most Likely Be Asked
52. Microsoft Excel Interview Questions You'll Most Likely Be Asked
53. Microsoft Powerpoint Interview Questions You'll Most Likely Be Asked
54. Microsoft Word Interview Questions You'll Most Likely Be Asked
55. MySQL Interview Questions You'll Most Likely Be Asked
56. NetSuite Interview Questions You'll Most Likely Be Asked
57. Networking Interview Questions You'll Most Likely Be Asked
58. OOPS Interview Questions You'll Most Likely Be Asked
59. Operating Systems Interview Questions You'll Most Likely Be Asked
60. Oracle DBA Interview Questions You'll Most Likely Be Asked
61. Oracle E-Business Suite Interview Questions You'll Most Likely Be Asked
62. ORACLE PL/SQL Interview Questions You'll Most Likely Be Asked
63. Perl Programming Interview Questions You'll Most Likely Be Asked
64. PHP Interview Questions You'll Most Likely Be Asked
65. PMP Interview Questions You'll Most Likely Be Asked
66. Python Interview Questions You'll Most Likely Be Asked
67. RESTful JAVA Web Services Interview Questions You'll Most Likely Be Asked
68. Ruby Interview Questions You'll Most Likely Be Asked
69. Ruby on Rails Interview Questions You'll Most Likely Be Asked
70. SAP ABAP Interview Questions You'll Most Likely Be Asked
71. SAP HANA Interview Questions You'll Most Likely Be Asked
72. SAS Programming Guidelines Interview Questions You'll Most Likely Be Asked
73. Selenium Testing Tools Interview Questions You'll Most Likely Be Asked
74. Silverlight Interview Questions You'll Most Likely Be Asked
75. Software Repositories Interview Questions You'll Most Likely Be Asked
76. Software Testing Interview Questions You'll Most Likely Be Asked
77. SQL Server Interview Questions You'll Most Likely Be Asked
78. Tomcat Interview Questions You'll Most Likely Be Asked
79. UML Interview Questions You'll Most Likely Be Asked
80. Unix Interview Questions You'll Most Likely Be Asked
81. UNIX Shell Programming Interview Questions You'll Most Likely Be Asked
82. VB.NET Interview Questions You'll Most Likely Be Asked
83. Windows Server 2008 R2 Interview Questions You'll Most Likely Be Asked
84. XLXP, XSLT, XPATH, XFORMS & XQuery Interview Questions You'll Most Likely Be Asked
85. XML Interview Questions You'll Most Likely Be Asked

For complete list visit

www.vibrantpublishers.com

Made in the USA
Middletown, DE
02 August 2017